The History of Nations

Canada

Other books in the History of Nations series:

THE HISTORY OF NATIONS

Canada

Nick Treanor, *Book Editor*

Daniel Leone, *President*
Bonnie Szumski, *Publisher*
Scott Barbour, *Managing Editor*

GREENHAVEN
PRESS ®

THOMSON

GALE

San Diego • Detroit • New York • San Francisco • Cleveland
New Haven, Conn. • Waterville, Maine • London • Munich

For more information, contact
Greenhaven Press
27500 Drake Rd.
Farmington Hills, MI 48331-3535
Or you can visit our Internet site at http://www.gale.com

LIBRARY OF CONGRESS CATALOGING-IN-PUBLICATION DATA

Canada / Nick Treanor, book editor.
    p. cm. — (History of nations)
  Includes bibliographical references and index.
  ISBN 0-7377-1192-2 (lib. : alk. paper) — ISBN 0-7377-1191-4 (pbk. : alk. paper)
    1. Canada—History. 2. Canada—Politics and government. 3. Canada—Ethnic
relations. I. Treanor, Nick. II. History of nations (Greenhaven Press)
  F1026 .C29 2003
  971—dc21   2002034725

Printed in the United States of America

Contents

Chapter 2: A Nation Comes of Age

Chapter 3: Two Solitudes: The French and the English

ciation between Canada and an independent Quebec would be best for the citizens of both countries.

Chapter 4: The Dream of the Just Society

costly, but recent cuts may serve to strengthen the system in the long run.

Chapter 5: Multiculturalism and the Future of Canada

Chapter 6: A Nation's Challenges

FOREWORD

In 1841, the journalist Charles MacKay remarked, "In reading the history of nations, we find that, like individuals, they have their whims and peculiarities, their seasons of excitement and recklessness." At the time of MacKay's observation, many of the nations explored in the Greenhaven Press History of Nations series did not yet exist in their current form. Nonetheless, whether it is old or young, every nation is similar to an individual, with its own distinct characteristics and unique story.

The History of Nations series is dedicated to exploring these stories. Each anthology traces the development of one of the world's nations from its earliest days, when it was perhaps no more than a promise on a piece of paper or an idea in the mind of some revolutionary, through to its status in the world today. Topics discussed include the pivotal political events and power struggles that shaped the country as well as important social and cultural movements. Often, certain dramatic themes and events recur, such as the rise and fall of empires, the flowering and decay of cultures, or the heroism and treachery of leaders. As well, in the history of most countries war, oppression, revolution, and deep social change feature prominently. Nonetheless, the details of such events vary greatly, as does their impact on the nation concerned. For example, England's "Glorious Revolution" of 1688 was a peaceful transfer of power that set the stage for the emergence of democratic institutions in that nation. On the other hand, in China, the overthrow of dynastic rule in 1912 led to years of chaos, civil war, and the eventual emergence of a Communist regime that used violence as a tool to root out opposition and quell popular protest. Readers of the Greenhaven Press History of Nations series will learn about the common challenges nations face and the different paths they take in response to such crises. However a nation's story may have developed, the series strives to present a clear and unbiased view of the country at hand.

The structure of each volume in the series is designed to help students deepen their understanding of the events, movements, and persons that define nations. First, a thematic introduction provides critical background material and helps orient the reader. The chapters themselves are designed to provide an accessible and engaging approach to the study of the history of that nation involved and are arranged either thematically or chronologically, as appropriate. The selections include both primary documents, which convey something of the flavor of the time and place concerned, and secondary material, which includes the wisdom of hindsight and scholarship. Finally, each book closes with a detailed chronology, a comprehensive bibliography of suggestions for further research, and a thorough index.

The countries explored within the series are as old as China and as young as Canada, as distinct in character as Spain and India, as large as Russia, and as compact as Japan. Some are based on ethnic nationalism, the belief in an ethnic group as a distinct people sharing a common destiny, whereas others emphasize civic nationalism, in which what defines citizenship is not ethnicity but commitment to a shared constitution and its values. As human societies become increasingly globalized, knowledge of other nations and of the diversity of their cultures, characteristics, and histories becomes ever more important. This series responds to the challenge by furnishing students with a solid and engaging introduction to the history of the world's nations.

INTRODUCTION

The history of Canada as a nation begins, oddly enough, with the American Revolution. This brief but urgent conflict is more commonly thought to mark the official birth of the United States, as well it does. And yet the American patriots, in wrenching the thirteen colonies from the hands of the British Empire, left the colonies north of the St. Lawrence River and the Great Lakes within that very empire. It is from these northern colonies, peopled at the time by French and English settlers, that the Canada of today has evolved.

Those who share François Voltaire's grim opinion of the northern half of the continent, which he dismissed in his 1759 work *Candide* as a "few acres of snow," might think that the thirteen colonies were hesitant to include in their young Union the northern colonies, which in those days had few people and fewer riches. The opposite, however, is true. Officials from the rebellious colonies of New England had tried, unsuccessfully, to persuade their northern neighbors to join the revolt against the British Crown.

Most of the northern population was French, remnants of the days when France sent its legendary *coureurs de bois,* or runners of the woods, to explore vast reaches of the continent by canoe and populated the banks of the St. Lawrence with *les habitants,* the peasant farmers. Although the population was largely French, the colony itself was British; Britain had recently bested France in the fight for the continent, and the 1763 Treaty of Paris had handed control to Britain. The American appeals to the northern colonies for assistance in the revolt against the Crown were unsuccessful not because the population there was staunchly loyal to the British, but because the largely French population was hesitant to form a nation with the overwhelmingly English-speaking Americans. For decades, the peasant population had worked the soil of the St. Lawrence lowlands and participated in parish and community life free from British interference, and it had little reason to upset the status quo. Furthermore, the Quebec Act, passed in 1774 by the British Parliament, had extended to the French

Catholics considerable protection of language and religion. As the historian Barry Gough has observed, "Paradoxically, Canada remained British because its inhabitants were French."[1]

Three Defining Forces

The refusal of the northern colonies to join the American revolt marks more than the beginning of Canada as a distinct nation. It also demonstrates the interplay of the three forces that have, throughout its history, shaped Canada as a nation. Unlike the United States, which was born suddenly in the battles of the War of Independence, Canada developed gradually. Its lengthy gestation was shaped by its enduring relationship to the expansive British Empire, by its relation to its powerful southern neighbor, and by the internal relations between its French and English peoples. These three crucial relationships, none of which existed independently of the others, together are responsible for Canada being the country it is today.

The Legacy of Empire

Through the Declaration of Independence and the ensuing war, in which Britain was unable to put down the colonists' revolt, the Americans got rid of the British once and for all. In contrast, more than two hundred years would pass before the last remaining colonial tie between the United Kingdom and Canada was cut. By then it was fair to say that it was the British who were getting rid of the Canadians rather than the other way around.

On a rainy day in April 1982, Queen Elizabeth II signed the Royal Proclamation patriating the Canadian constitution. Until that moment, the Canadian constitution, known as the British North America Act of 1867, could only be amended by an act of the British Parliament. The patriation of the constitution, however, meant that for the first time the Canadian government, without the consent or approval of Britain, had the power to change its own constitution, the basic law that provides the legal framework for a country's existence as a political entity. As Canadian prime minister Pierre Trudeau remarked at the proclamation ceremony, the long delay in severing the last remaining colonial tie had not been due to British reluctance. More than fifty years earlier, with the Statute of Westminster, the British Parliament had granted effective independence to Canada and other dominions within its empire. Only Canada, however, did not receive the power to change its own constitution, and that was by its own deliberate request. The request was motivated by the fact that the federal and provincial governments, at the time of the Statute of Westminster, had been unable to agree on what is known rather dryly as an "amending formula." (Essentially, what was at issue was the balance of power between the federal and provincial governments, and especially the role of Quebec, which saw itself as deserving special status in virtue of its being a French minority and a founding people.)

Although it would be a mistake to think of present-day Canada as an essentially British nation given the enduring French presence and the country's multicultural population, Canada's gradual evolution within the British Empire and Commonwealth has left a distinctive mark. For one thing, Canadians have an attitude toward government that is quite different from that of their southern neighbors. The United States was born in revolt, and its constitution and persona demonstrate a suspicion of large governments and an emphasis on individual rather than communal rights and goods. The American colonists, in rejecting the British Crown, were rejecting undemocratic authority. Canada, in contrast, never felt compelled to reject the monarchial system; although it gradually developed into a full-fledged democracy, it did so, for the most part, without developing suspicion toward powerful central government.

The Role of Government

The imperial system, however it may be faulted on democratic grounds, was one in which, in principle at least, the sovereign made decisions motivated by the good of the empire and the welfare of his or her subjects. Just as the subjects were to be loyal to the sovereign, the sovereign was to serve the good of the people. Although the Canadian political structure has mostly abandoned this imperial system, something of its spirit survives. Canadians tend to expect their government to act in their interest by providing nationalized health care, public schools and universities, extensive welfare, unemployment insurance and pensions, and a host of other services. Furthermore, public works projects initiated by the government, such as transcontinental railroads and communications systems, played a major role in determining the shape of national development. Additionally, Crown corporations were expected to offer essential services that could not be profitably offered by private enterprise. Finally, the idea that parts of an empire support each other survives in the Canadian system of transfer payments, by which the federal government directs tax revenues from wealthy provinces, such as Ontario and Alberta, toward less affluent provinces, such as those on the Atlantic coast.

This difference between American and Canadian views of government is reflected in the countries' respective national slogans. The United States, honoring its commitment to individualism, emphasizes "life, liberty, and the pursuit of happiness." Canada, in contrast, stresses communal responsibility by emphasizing "peace, order, and good government." The contrast is a direct result of the quite different experience each nation had with the British Empire.

The Structure of Government

The connection between Canada and the United Kingdom, which endures in the form of the Commonwealth, affected more than just Canadians' attitudes toward government. The structure of Canada's government is also inherited from the British. As John A. Macdonald, who became Canada's first prime minister, remarked in a conference on confederation in 1864, "I think we had better return to the original principle and in the words of Governor Simcoe, endeavour to make ours 'an image and transcript of the British Constitution.'"[2] Thus, Canada has a House of Commons rather than a Congress and a prime minister rather than a president. Furthermore, although in both the United States and Canada the role of the Senate is to provide a sober second look at legislation passed by the lower house, the Canadian Senate, unlike its American counterpart, is not elected for terms. Instead, senators are appointed for life terms by the governor general, the queen's representative in Canada, on the advice of the Canadian prime minister. Politically, such a system is partway between the elected American Senate and the traditional House of Lords in Britain.

In addition to affecting the development of Canada's political systems, Canada's relationship with the United Kingdom affected its economic development. Within the British imperial system, the role of colonies, such as Canada, was to send raw materials to Britain and buy back finished manufactured goods. Consequently, Canadian economic development focused on harvesting natural resources. In the earliest days of the colony, the commodity of choice was fur; later fish, lumber, and eventually minerals and oil became most important. Unlike the United States, manufacturing in Canada was very slow to develop and was even stifled by British regulations that were designed to protect industries in English cities from competition. Canada eventually developed a strong industrial base, but the emphasis on natural resource exploitation remains. Today, for instance, Canada exports more timber than any other country.

The Spoils of War

Since 1867, when the British North America Act created the Dominion of Canada (the first and most important step toward the full and final independence achieved by the 1982 patriation), the Canadian government rather than the British Parliament has made most decisions concerning the governance of the country. Nonetheless, the loyalties between English Canada and the Crown continued to run deep. At no time was Canada's connection to the United Kingdom more pronounced than during World Wars I and II. Over one hundred thousand Canadian soldiers died in the two world wars, perishing in the dark trenches of Flanders, over the rough waters of the English Channel, and on the unwelcoming beaches of Normandy. Although in neither war was Canada itself ever seriously threatened, in both wars it was understood that the young country would come to the defense of the old. In 1914 Canada was at war the moment Britain was; there was no need for a separate declaration of war. By 1939, in contrast, Canada waited a full week longer than Britain to declare war on Germany, and in so doing it asserted its independence as a nation. (This delay also let the administration of Franklin Delano Roosevelt exploit a loophole in the United States' neutrality legislation so that it could export crucial military aircraft to Canada.) With much of the important natural resources of Europe, especially iron, cut off from the Allies by hostile armies, production of Canadian mining, timber, and food resources boomed. So too did industrial production, and by 1945 Canada was able to record its first trade surplus with the United States. Although Canada entered each war because it was a part of the British Empire, both times Canada's wartime sacrifices boosted its status on the world stage as an independent country. In 1919, for instance, Canada had its own signature on the Versailles peace treaty. In 1943 Prime Minister

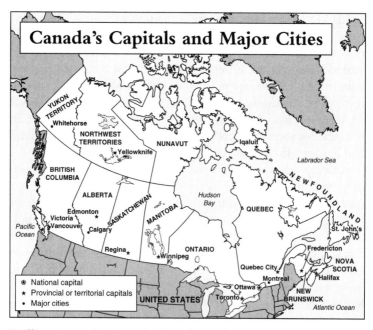

Canada's Capitals and Major Cities

* National capital
* Provincial or territorial capitals
* Major cities

William Lyon Mackenzie King hosted a meeting in Quebec of U.S. president Franklin Roosevelt, British prime minister Winston Churchill, and China's foreign minister T.V. Soong to discuss the Allied war effort. The following year, again at Quebec, King hosted Roosevelt, Churchill, and their chief military advisers in order to discuss the future of Germany, whose defeat was imminent. After the war, Canada's status as a middle power was further secured by its playing a major role in the creation of the United Nations, with a Canadian, John Humphrey, even being the principal author of the Universal Declaration of Human Rights. Although Canada had entered the war a loyal child of Britain, it concluded the war Britain's able peer.

One Country, Two Peoples

If Canada's participation in the two world wars demonstrated its close relationship to Britain, the fierce debate within the country over that participation demonstrated the second of the crucial relationships that have shaped Canada through its history: the relation between the English and the French in Canada. At the start of each war, the government was able to successfully recruit, train, and equip enough volunteers (both English and French). As the wars progressed, however, and dead and wounded soldiers needed to be replaced with fresh recruits, the supply of volunteers dried up and the government began to consider conscription. Each time, French Canadians fiercely resisted and deeply resented conscription. Quebec saw little reason to ship its sons, against their will, to face possible death in a war that had, as far as they were considered, little to do with Quebec. Canada was fighting because the British were fighting, and the French in Canada, not surprisingly, felt little loyalty toward the British who had defeated their ancestors at the Plains of Abraham in 1758.

Although the relationship between the English and the French in Canada had never been perfectly smooth, the bitter fight over conscription tore open old wounds and reminded the Québécois of their vulnerability as a minority within the Canadian confederation. In 1774, when the British Parliament passed the Quebec Act to protect French rights in Canada, most of the European inhabitants of what was to become Canada were French. Soon, however, waves of English-speaking immigrants from the United States and Europe reduced the French to a minority, and it was clear that most colonial rulers looked forward to the day when the French would be assimilated, adopting the English language and Anglo-American customs. Indeed, Lord Durham, in an 1839 report to the British Parliament on the state of the English and French colonies, had urged assimilation, saying it was necessary if the French were to prosper. Furthermore, Durham reported that he had found in Canada "two nations warring in the bosom of a single state," and he warned that only assimilation would bring tranquility. Were Durham alive during the early decades of the twentieth century, he might have been surprised to discover that the French, far from being assimilated, had successfully maintained their language and customs. One of the chief reasons for this was the phenomenal birthrate within Quebec, which ensured continuous strong population growth. The other important reason, however, was that Quebec remained something of an isolated society, where life remained centered on the local parish and farming community.

The Fear of Assimilation

Just as the fight over conscription reminded the Québécois of their vulnerability, the expanding transportation and communication networks of the twentieth century were increasingly bringing the English-speaking continent into their lives. Modernity arrived late in Quebec, but when it did it was accompanied by the perils of assimilation. In this atmosphere, a renewed sense of nationalism emerged, and by the late 1960s prominent Quebec politicians were pursuing sovereignty for Quebec. The country that was envisioned by its founders as stretching "from sea to shining sea" was in danger of having its largest province separate and form a nation of its own.

In 1980, 60 percent of Quebec voters rejected sovereignty in a provincial referendum, but that did not put an end to the hopes of Quebec nationalists. In 1995 a second referendum was held in Quebec, and this time just 51 percent of voters rejected separation. It is hard to say whether the narrower margin represented the growth of separatist sentiment in Quebec or merely the contingencies of that 1995 referendum, but what is clear is that a significant proportion of Quebecers do not feel fully at home within the Canadian confederation. Indeed, during the 1990s the Bloc Québécois, a separatist party, swept Quebec during the federal election and won the second-greatest number of seats in Parliament. Canadians, both French and English, were ruled by a parliament in which a separatist party played the role of "Her Majesty's Loyal Opposition," as the party with the second-greatest number of seats is known in the Canadian political system. To many observers, the situation would have been comical if it had not been so serious.

Although the enduring presence of two language and cultural groups in Canada has led, on occasion, to misunderstanding and resentment, it has also left a positive mark on the national consciousness. Canadians for the most part take pride in the fact that disagreements between the French and the English have been, with rare exceptions, addressed with words rather than with weapons. Indeed, in recent years several European countries have studied the Canadian model in an attempt to understand and manage the difficulties that inevitably arise in culturally diverse societies. The Canadian model stresses the collective rights of identifiable minorities, in contrast to the traditional liberal model in which every individual has equal and identical rights. For instance, the French language is protected in Quebec through a law that limits the use of English on public signs and store fronts. In some societies, such a law would be considered an obvious encroachment on individual liberty. To its Canadian defenders, however, this law affords legitimate protection to a threatened minority. Whether or not one accepts that minorities may have special rights of their own, it is clear that Canada's bicultural history has affected its understanding of individual versus collective rights.

Patriotism and National Identity

Canada's long colonial relationship with the United Kingdom and French Canadians' dissatisfaction with their role as a minority group have together affected Canadian patriotism. Until recently, it was rare to see or hear public displays of patriotism in Canada, and as the Canadian journalist Robert Fulford notes, "Being patriotic is not a prerequisite of Canadian citizenship."[3] Unlike the United States, which was founded on a creed of individualism and liberty and expects its citizens' allegiance to those principles, Canada lacks a defining mythology; there is no such thing as being un-Canadian. In recent years, however, overt displays of national affection have become more common. Many Canadians have come to view multicultural diversity and compassionate government as defining national features, however imperfectly they may be fulfilled.

Political and social commentators in Canada never tire of discussing the question of national identity or of pointing out how interminable such a discussion is. For most of its history as a country, Canada was never quite sure of what it was. So close were its imperial ties to the United Kingdom that it did not consider itself a wholly independent country, and yet it was too French to be wholly British. One thing everyone could agree on, however, was that Canada was not American.

Canada's Continental Neighbor

Since the founding of the United States, its presence and its power have exerted a tremendous effect on the development of Canada. Sometimes this influence came in the form of cross-border trade in goods, ideas, and culture. Just as often, however, the influence came in the form of Canadian political decisions that were based on the threat of invasion or assimilation by Americans.

During the years immediately following the American Revolution, tens of thousands of United Empire Loyalists migrated to Canada from the young republic. This was the first significant wave of English-speaking settlers, and because they had often been driven out of the United States by persecution, most harbored suspicion and resentment toward their southern neighbors.

Those suspicions were confirmed in 1812, when American brigadier general William Hull and his troops crossed the Detroit River to land at Windsor. Thomas Jefferson had declared that a successful invasion of Canada would be a "mere matter of marching," but by 1814 the Americans had been driven out, Washington was occupied, and the president's house was in flames. The war ended in stalemate, and the border returned to its prewar position.

Although the Canadian colony had successfully resisted the invasion, there was no doubt that this was due solely to the British troops furnished by King George III. There was also no doubt that the Americans, although their attention was now directed toward conquering the West, still had their eye on the northern half of the continent. Indeed, by the 1840s the American policy of manifest destiny announced that the entire continent was to belong to the United States. As one newspaper editor put it, "Other nations have tried to check . . . the fulfillment of our manifest destiny to overspread the continent allotted by Providence for the free development of our yearly multiplying millions."[4] The Canadian colonies, however, which had not volunteered to join in the American Revolution in 1775, were even more reluctant to be converted against their will more than half a century later.

By the mid-1800s, Britain had found that managing the Canadian colonies, which in those days lay almost entirely east of Lake Michigan, had become too costly. The colonies, with their long winters, could barely produce enough food for their own population, let alone for the population of the British Isles as the hope had once been. Britain was also concerned that as long as it maintained colonies on the North American continent, it would be obliged to defend them from the Americans. Gradually, helped along in no small part by the British, a plan for Canadian confederation took shape in which Ontario, Quebec, Nova Scotia, and New Brunswick would join to form a largely self-governing dominion. During the 1860s, in particular, Britain was concerned about the Fenians, as militant Irish nationalists in the United States were known. The Fenians, many of whom returned from the Civil War with honed fighting skills, intended to capture the Canadian colonies and hold them for ransom in return for Ireland. Although there is some controversy among historians about how seriously Britain took the Fenian threat, there is little doubt that the Canadian Confederation of 1867 was at least to some degree a response to perceived threats south of the border. Britain had been gradually withdrawing its troops, and in 1861 only two thousand remained in Canada. By converting Canada from an assortment of colonies to a country, Britain was able to bring home the rest of its soldiers, and by 1871 only a few British troops remained in Canada at a naval base in Halifax. Henceforth, the defense of Canada would be up to the Canadians.

The Race to the West

As the nineteenth century progressed, Canadian fears about armed American invasion declined. But a new kind of worry arose. The vast reaches of the Canadian west, from the Great Lakes to the Pacific Ocean, were empty of settlers; with few exceptions, the first nations (as Indians in Canada are known) and the Métis, the descendants of French Canadian explorers and Native American mothers, were the only inhabitants. Americans had long been aggressively settling their western territories, pushing past the Mississippi in long caravans, and by the latter half of the century they began moving north, into the plains east of the Rocky Mountains. The Canadian government, concerned about losing its western territories, began to focus on populating the West. To this end, ambitious national railroad projects were started, the goal of which was to lay track all the way to Vancouver. These projects commanded much of the national attention, bolstered at times by propaganda from the railroad industry that focused on the hardships railroads could be expected to ease:

> Old winter is once more upon us, and our inland seas are "dreary and inhospitable wastes" to the merchant and to the traveler;—our rivers are sealed fountains— and an embargo which no human power can remove is laid on all our ports.... Far to the South is heard the daily scream of the steam-whistle—but from Canada there is no escape: blockaded and imprisoned by Ice and Apathy, we have at least ample time for reflection.[5]

In addition, at the turn of the century a new immigration policy opened up the West to European emigrants, who traveled by railroad directly from the port of Montreal to the burgeoning prairies. Those new Canadians, a large contingent of whom had been raised to farm the fertile Ukrainian steppe, quickly transformed the prairies. In 1900, for example, Saskatoon consisted of a general store. Two years later, perhaps twenty houses counted as a village. Three years later it was a city, and in 1911 the census counted twelve thousand people, a university, and two transcontinental railroads. Nor was the experience in Saskatoon uncommon—not including first nations and Métis, the population west of Ontario in 1911 was one hundred times greater than it had been in 1870. This tremendous growth was a direct result of concerns about American encroachment, and besides populating the West, it introduced to Canada the first significant immigrant population that stemmed from neither the United Kingdom nor France.

The Undefended Border

During the twentieth century the chief ways in which the United States influenced the development of Canada were in terms of economics, defense, and culture. Given that Canada's population has always been only about one-tenth that of the United States, and given the sheer volume of U.S. economic and cultural production, it was inevitable that much of both would spill over into Canada. Likewise, given Canada's proximity to the United States, and the fact that it sat between the United States and its cold war enemy, the Soviet Union, it was natural for the United States to take a keen interest in issues of Canadian defense.

The volume of trade between Canada and the United States is the largest between any two countries in the world. Because the Canadian economy is much smaller than that of the United States, however, trade between the two countries makes up a correspondingly larger proportion of the Canadian economy. Consequently, Canada is much more vulnerable to fluctuations in the U.S. economy as well as to changes in border tariffs. In fact, in 1969 Prime Minister Pierre Trudeau joked in an address to an American audience at the National Press Club in Washington that "living next to you is in some ways like sleeping with an elephant. No matter how friendly and even-tempered is the beast, if I can call it that, one is affected by every twitch and grunt."[6] The U.S. impact on Canada's economy has been manifold. Canadian businesses have traditionally had to keep a close eye on trends within the American market. At times the United States has also been able to use its trade leverage to its advantage during disagreements on tariffs or industry subsidies. Furthermore, when British colonial policies stunted the growth of industry in

Canada, large American firms were often able to fill the gap by opening branch plants, especially in Ontario. This brought industry to Canada, and consequently employment, but the ownership was foreign. This early trend toward foreign ownership of industry has continued, even as Canadian industry has developed. Finally, of course, powerful American retail chains such as Wal-Mart and Starbucks have stepped in to compete with the home-grown Hudson's Bay Company, a department store descended from the fur trading company, and Tim Horton's, a popular coffee and doughnut shop founded by a member of the National Hockey League. The 1994 North American Free Trade Agreement between Canada, the United States, and Mexico has deepened this economic interconnectedness, to the chagrin of many Canadians who insist the deal threatens Canadian jobs and the country's political independence.

The Canadian Military

The United States has also had a profound impact on Canada's military. Throughout the Cold War, Canada sat in the firing line between the United States and the Soviet Union and was involved in several joint ventures with Americans, such as the distant early warning radar network, which monitored activity in Canada's northern airspace. Perhaps most significantly, however, given the huge American military buildup after World War II, the stated American intention of defending the hemisphere, and Canada's participation in the North Atlantic Treaty Organization, there has been little reason for Canada to pour a lot of money into its military. Canada could not repel a U.S. invasion, but Canadians could also be certain that in the tense atmosphere of the cold war any other country trying to invade Canada would most likely meet stiff American resistance. Consequently, although Canada had one of the largest militaries in the world in 1945, it underwent a massive decommissioning of arms in the decades that followed, freeing up that portion of its budget for other projects. Soon, most Canadians would come to take a certain amount of pleasure in having a weak and poorly funded military, holding it to be a national virtue rather than a vice. This attitude was bolstered when Canadian prime minister Lester B. Pearson won the Nobel Peace Prize in 1957 for helping to defuse the Suez Canal crisis. Henceforth, at least in popular mythology, Canada would take peacekeeping and diplomacy to be its mission abroad.

Staying Canadian

In cultural terms, the influence of the United States became most pronounced with the advent of mass communications, particularly radio, television, and magazines. The vast majority of the Canadian population is huddled along the American border at the very south of the country, where radios and televisions have little trouble picking up American stations. As a result, in addition to stifling the development of Canadian cultural content, the ready availability of American productions meant that Canadians came to know much about the United States, and sometimes even more about the United States than about their own country.

In recent decades, in fact, the traditional Canadian concern about assimilation has manifested principally as resistance to some of the American ideals and norms that drift across the border on television, radio, and in print. In particular, Canadians tend to frown on what they see as religious fundamentalism, lingering racism, conservative political attitudes, inadequate social spending, military jingoism, and high crime and harsh punishment south of the border. Just as in 1776, when the colonists in what is now Canada chose not to join the American Revolution, Canadians today, however much they may admire certain things about the United States, tend to be adamant about not becoming too much like Americans. As the historian Frank Underhill remarks, Canadians

> made the great refusal in 1776 when they declined to join the revolting American colonies. They made it again in 1812 when they repelled American invaders. They made it again in 1837 when they rejected a revolution motivated by ideals of Jacksonian democracy, and opted instead for a staid moderate respectable British Whiggism which they called "Responsible Government". They made it once more in 1867 when the separate British colonies joined to set up a new nationality in order to preempt [American] expansionism.[7]

Underhill also has said of the Canadian efforts to resist the Americanization of the country, "It would be hard to overestimate the amount of energy we have devoted to this cause."[8] This devotion continues; therefore, one of the chief ways in which the United States affects Canada is by serving as a model against which Canadians can forge a national identity.

The Face of Canada Today

Shaped by the British, the French, and the Americans, Canada to-day reaches from the Grand Banks of Newfoundland, where teeming schools of cod first widened European eyes, to the Pacific Coast, where Douglas firs tower three hundred feet over misty fiords, to the frozen archipelago of the north, where in summer the sun never sets. Most of the native people who were able to survive gunpowder and smallpox, both of which crossed the Atlantic in the bellies of European ships, have long since been displaced to reservations, although in recent years there have been renewed discussions of native land claims, and a vast new territory in the north, Nunavut, has been created as a place for Inuit self-governance.

The ten provinces and three territories that today compose Canada divide rather neatly into six regions. In the east, Newfoundland, Prince Edward Island, Nova Scotia, and New Brunswick form the Maritimes, where fishing, lumber, and mining are core industries. Next, Quebec looms northward from the fertile soil of the St. Lawrence River Valley for nearly twelve hundred miles, the great majority of which are empty except for wood and water and rock, and the logging trucks, hydroelectric dams, and mines that exploit these resources. West of Quebec is Ontario, the industrial engine of the country and home to one-third of Canadians. As in Quebec, its population is clustered for the most part in the temperate south, and logging and mining are important northern industries, although they compete with recreational canoeists and campers seeking refuge from the cities of the south. To the west of Ontario come the prairie provinces of Manitoba, Saskatchewan, and Alberta, where endless fields of grain, huge herds of cattle, and oil extraction form the backbone of the economy. Along the west coast, sharing the Rocky Mountains with Alberta, is British Columbia, home to 50 percent of Canada's forestry industry and to the port of Vancouver, gateway to the Pacific Rim. Finally, in the north, the Yukon Territory, the Northwest Territories, and, since 1999, Nunavut form a frozen desert. The tiny population here consists mostly of those who work in natural resource extraction and of the Inuit, whom the extremes of climate and distance have somewhat protected from disruption and interference. As Prime Minister William Lyon Mackenzie King remarked in a speech in the House of Commons in 1936, "If some countries have too much history, [Canada] has too much geography."[9]

Despite this picture of a vast country in which miners, foresters, and farmers are important, most Canadians today live in industrialized cities. In fact, the three largest cities of Toronto, Montreal, and Vancouver alone are home to nearly one-third of Canadians. Increasingly, Canadians are looking to their cities as the centers of growth and development, and the urban population, fueled by high rates of immigration, continues to boom. Since 1971 Canada has had an official policy of multiculturalism, which encourages new immigrants to retain aspects of their cultural identities. In the prevailing metaphor, this has converted most major cities from staid English or French preserves to multicultural mosaics. Indeed, although the French in Canada continue to be concerned about losing their culture and identity, it is Canada's British descendants who have lost much of their culture and many of their traditions. In cities such as Toronto, where over half the population was born outside of Canada, lunch is far more likely to consist of pad thai, tikka marsala, or sushi than it is to include shortbread and scones. The influence of Canada's long history as part of the British Empire remains, of course, but during the twenty-first century the relationships that will most shape the country are likely to be those between English and French Canadians, between Canada and the United States, and between native Canadians and new immigrants. The effects of these relationships are hard to predict.

Notes

1. Barry Gough, *Canada*. Englewood Cliffs, NJ: Prentice-Hall, 1975, p. 38.
2. Quoted in Sir J. Pope, *Memoirs of the Rt. Hon. Sir John A. Macdonald*, vol. 1. Toronto: Oxford University Press, 1930, p. 286.
3. Quoted in Peter C. Newman, *True North: Not Strong and Free*. Toronto: McClelland and Stewart, 1983, p. 29.
4. John Louis O'Sullivan, editorial in *U.S. Magazine and Democratic Review*, July/August 1845, vol. 17.
5. Thomas Coltrin Keefer, *Philosophy of Railroads*. Montreal: Order of the Directors of the St. Lawrence and Ottawa Grand Junction Railroad Company, 1853, p. 3.
6. Pierre Trudeau, quoted on the *Globe and Mail* website, www.globeandmail.com.
7. Frank Underhill, *In Search of Canadian Liberalism*. Toronto: Macmillan of Canada, 1960, p. 222.
8. Underhill, *In Search of Canadian Liberalism*, p. 222.
9. Quoted in Seymour Martin Lipset, *Continental Divide*. New York: Routledge, 1990, p. 56.

From Conquest to Confederation

Indians and Europeans at the Time of Contact

By J.R. Miller

In the following selection, University of Saskatchewan history professor J.R. Miller discusses early contact between Europeans and native communities in Canada, focusing on how the social and cultural characteristics of each group shaped and determined their interaction. The native peoples of Canada were highly diversified societies with social customs and institutions that were very different from those of the European explorers, missionaries, and settlers they encountered in the 1500s. According to Miller, the Europeans tended to expect coercion to figure prominently in political relations, had more acquisitive economies, and were motivated by religious principles that gave them a duty to spread their faith. Additionally, Miller describes how much of the details of European settlement reflected historical contingencies, such as the fact that English and French fishermen, unlike the Spaniards and Basques, didn't have a ready supply of salt from home and thus had to stay ashore on the newly discovered continent for extended periods in order to dry and salt their fish.

O n 24 July after more than a week of observing and bartering with the native inhabitants, the newcomers set about erecting a landmark at the mouth of the harbour on the Bay of Chaleur. Jacques Cartier's men

> had a cross made thirty feet high, which was put together in the presence of a number of the Indians on the point at the entrance to this harbour, under the cross-bar of which we fixed a shield with three *fleurs-de-lys* in relief, and above it a wooden board, engraved in large Gothic characters, where was written, LONG

J.R. Miller, *Skyscrapers Hide the Heavens: A History of Indian-White Relations in Canada.* Toronto: University of Toronto Press, 1989. Copyright © 1989 by University of Toronto Press. Reproduced by permission.

LIVE THE KING OF FRANCE. We erected this cross on the point in their presence and they watched it being put together and set up.

When we had returned to our ships, the chief, dressed in an old black bear-skin, arrived in a canoe with three of his sons and his brother; but they did not come so close to the ships as they had usually done. And pointing to the cross he [the chief] made us a long harangue, making the sign of the cross with two of his fingers; and then he pointed to the land all around about, as if he wished to say that all this region belonged to him, and that we ought not to have set up this cross without his permission.

The encounter of Micmac and Frenchmen at Gaspé in July 1534 contained many of the elements of early relations between natives and intruders. The French explored, traded, and attempted to leave their permanent mark on the place. The Indians happily bartered but rejected the white men's presumption at erecting a signpost. This epitome of early relations was all the more remarkable because it brought together two dramatically different peoples, two contrasting societies that would nonetheless cooperate successfully for centuries before relations deteriorated into conflict and confrontation.

Diverse Native Communities

The aboriginal societies with whom Cartier and those who followed him came into contact were diverse and well established in their respective territories. Their ancestors had entered North America from Siberia by way of the Bering Strait in search of game perhaps as long as 40,000 years ago. Sometime in the subsequent millennia they had made their way southward, in part following a path in the lee of the continental spine formed by the Rockies and Sierras, and diffused throughout the continent. Evidence of what were undoubtedly the original human occupiers of the continent that was unearthed in the Yukon indicates that they were there as long as 27,000 years ago.

These peoples began to diffuse into the northeastern part of the continent approximately 12,000 years ago. As the glaciers retreated northward at the end of the last ice age, humans migrated after them in search of fish, game, and arable land in which to cultivate a few crops that they had developed further south. Chief among these agricultural products was maize or corn, which was being grown and harvested a thousand years ago in the territory that at present is southern Ontario and Quebec. Other groups of aboriginal peoples who lived north of the arable land, in the Precambrian Shield or the colder regions to the north of that, were more dependent on hunting and fishing. Naturally, those peoples who migrated to the eastern seaboard developed an extensive fishery, which they supplemented with hunting and gathering of berries and nuts. In short, long before the European intruded in North America the indigenous peoples had entered and diffused into many parts of the continent, in the process showing an impressive ability to adapt to local climatic, topographical, and ecological conditions. . . .

Indian communities . . . were highly diversified societies of people who had adapted to their environment and worked out a code of behaviour for living compatibly with their world. There was no monolith called 'Indian.' There was wide variety depending on the topography and fauna of the region in which the people lived and the consequent nature of their economy. The Indian nations that occupied the northeastern part of North America 600 years ago had evolved to accommodate themselves to their world and to one another. Their values and institutions were still experiencing slow change at the time of the first contact with Europeans. Though they had pronounced differences, they also shared some features. They participated in some activities, such as commerce and warfare, and thereby learned of different ways. Their theology and ethics were roughly similar. But in spite of these significant similarities, it made little sense to regard them as one, undifferentiated human community. To label all the indigenous peoples simply 'Indians' and treat them as though they were the same made about as much sense as naming all newcomers 'Europeans' and pretending that there were not sharp differences among them. Any newcomers to North America would have to take the distinctive nature of Indian societies into consideration; immigrants, too, would have to adjust.

The Arriving Europeans

It was not 'Europeans' who came to North America but Basque whalers, west-country English fishermen, Dutch traders, and French missionaries. Though it would take the indigenous populations some time to understand this diversity, the differences among the intruders were pronounced, and their different natures and purposes had much to do with the type of relations they established with the inhabitants of the continent they began to reach in the late fifteenth century. And yet, like aboriginal communities, the Europeans had common features that united them and distinguished them from the Indians. These included their social and economic structures, their political systems, and their beliefs.

European societies of the sixteenth century were highly stratified and their governments were coercive in nature. In all the Western European states there was a well-established hierarchy of nobles, gentry, burghers, and common people. Though those of higher rank could have obligations to the less fortunate, individualism was more deeply ingrained among them than it was among the peoples of North America. The ethic of sharing was not as important and all-pervasive among these European peoples as it was in North American societies. Their polities, though they varied in detail, all employed coercion to enforce decisions. Absolutism was firmly entrenched in some countries, while the beginnings of parliamentary government were stirring in others. But in all it was expected that policy, once arrived at by debate or fiat, would be enforced. The king's troops, the local militia, or the community's tiny police force would impose the decisions of court, parliament, or magistrates on people. From the standpoint of those that gave the orders for enforcement, the only problem was that military and police power did not reach nearly as far as the ambitions of the rulers. Often what freedom people enjoyed in these societies was a function of the inability of the powerful to exert coercive power effectively.

European countries were not just structured societies and authoritarian polities; they were also acquisitive economies. By the sixteenth century the beginnings of a market mentality could be detected in some of them, particularly Holland and England. The significance of capitalism lay in its psychological character: capitalists both acted on and promoted a desire to acquire material goods, not simply for consumption and other social purposes but for reinvestment for the purpose of acquiring still more property. This economic motive also encouraged the development of an individualistic spirit that was beginning in economically advanced countries to erode communal ties of village loyalty and clan solidarity. In time this impulse, strengthened by the individualistic intellectual traditions that were a product of the European Renaissance, would remake the social ethics of Europe. The same forces, abetted by economic motivation, were bringing about a new reliance on machine technology and novel forms of energy. This revolution, like the impact of the Renaissance and the expanding grip of capitalist ethics, was turning Western Europe into an increasingly individualistic and acquisitive human community. At its best this process would lead to considerable prosperity and a high degree of personal liberty; at its worst to unbridled selfishness and yawning chasms between affluent and poor.

Though the Western European countries had economies that were diversified, and though the primary economic ambitions of these peoples differed widely, there were but a few economic reasons for the Europeans' approach to North America. After the era of abortive Norse exploration and settlement, the first contacts were made by fishing boats sometime in the fifteenth century. Although many European countries sought protein in the waters of North America, the Basques, Spanish, French, and English emerged as the most numerous and prominent of the fishermen off Newfoundland and Nova Scotia. They were in search especially of whales and cod, which were found in incredible profusion on the Grand Banks.

Although the fishing boats of the various European countries all sought mainly the same product, they would do different things with it. By an accident of geography and history, fishermen were forced to ply their trade in different ways in North America. Those from the more southerly regions had quantities of solar salt that they could use to preserve the fish on board their vessels before returning to Europe. Those from more northerly areas, particularly Normans, Bretons, and English, did not have access to a supply of salt from the Bay of Biscay. They could not use the 'green fishery' of their southern competitors, but had to follow the dry fishery. As a result, Europeans from more northerly countries began the practice of landing for protracted periods to erect the stands on which they dried the cod they had cleaned before packing it on board ship for the return voyage. These stays ashore meant that they came into contact, and conflict, with the indigenous inhabitants to a much greater extent than those who landed less frequently for shorter periods in search of fresh water, food, and wood for repairs. If the contact with aboriginal peoples in the future Canada revolved around northern French and British rather than Spaniards and Basques, the explanation lies to a great extent in whose home territory yielded salt evaporated from sea water and whose did not.

European and Native Cooperation

In time, and for reasons that will be explained later, this first contact led to an extensive commercial relationship between Europeans and coastal Algonkians such as the Micmac. Occasional visits of fishermen produced meetings; meetings led to barter of tools and clothing for furs; and out of these encounters grew the second major Canadian economy of the European era, the fur trade. Two important aspects of both the fish and the fur trades helped to shape the ensuing relationship of European and Indian: the European was motivated by the desire for gain; and achievement of his economic goal required the cooperation of the indigenous peoples with whom he came into contact.

There were two other principal motives for European expansion to North America in the fifteenth and sixteenth centuries—exploration and proselytization. Europeans knew from the accounts of Marco Polo's voyages to the lands of the Great Khan and from other even more fabulous accounts that regions with great riches in the form of spices and precious metals lay in the east. Thanks to the discoveries of science and the speculations of navigators, it was thinkable and feasible to sail west in hopes of finding these riches. Many of the early European explorers, in part at least, sailed to North America in search of Asia. Some of them thought that these western lands were the east, as the application of the term 'Indians' to the people of what explorers thought at first were the Indies graphically illustrates. Navigators and ship captains in the fifteenth and sixteenth centuries probed westward in search of the Orient, and, later, when they realized that North America was not Asia, in hopes of finding a waterway through this land mass to the lands of the Khan. They, too, like the fishing-boat captain and the fur trader who followed in his wake, would discover that they needed the cooperation of the indigenous peoples whom they encountered on their voyages of exploration.

Finally, there was also a non-monetary reason for European countries to send people to North America from the seventeenth century onward: religion. Europe was Christian, and from that simple social fact many important consequences followed. For one thing, Christians, like the Hebrews from whom they were historically and theologically descended, held a worldview that contrasted sharply with the animistic beliefs of the indigenous peoples of North America. Amerindians believed that they were only one species among many. An Indian's spirit was but one among a myriad of spirits of people, animals, fish, flora, and minerals. In contrast, Christians believed that they held a special place in creation. At the irreducible core of Christianity was the dictum that God created man in the deity's image, and that the non-human world was available for human use and God's glorification. While Christianity recognized a duty of stewardship in the use and exploitation of the non-human things that God had put on earth for Christians' advantage, it also confirmed that human beings were on a higher level of existence than animals, fish, and the rest of the natural world. This worldview had fuelled Western society's development of science and subjugation of nature by means of technology ever since the Renaissance. By the sixteenth century it had so shaped Christians' attitudes that they saw themselves as the more important part of a duality—humans and nature. It was an interpretation of reality and the place of human beings in creation that differed fundamentally from that of the indigenous populations of North America.

The significance of religion to the early contact between Europeans and aborigines did not end with Christianity's influence on the European view of the world; Christianity also had a bearing on which European peoples would undertake the exploration and economic development of the northern part of what would later be known as North America. The Vatican had decreed that all new lands were to be divided by the Christian nations of Spain and Portugal. Francis I of France did not accept his exclusion from the potential riches of the Western Hemisphere. 'Show me Adam's will!' he is supposed to have said of the papal edict. In practice, France secured Rome's acquiescence in French efforts to find new lands to the north of those already being exploited by the Iberian states. It was politic and convenient to direct most of the voyages that the French crown sponsored to the northerly latitudes. So, in part, it was that the French concentrated many of their attentions on the region that would later become Canada. Certainly that was true of state-sponsored evangelical efforts, which were themselves another manifestation of the Christian nature of Europe.

A Renewed Catholicism

It was a historically important coincidence that much of the early period of European exploration and penetration of North America was an era of intense religious feeling. The Catholic church had been wracked and divided by a drive for reform led by those who protested against the spiritual flabbiness and fleshly venality of an institution that had held a monopoly of religious services for centuries. The emergence of various forms of Protestantism would play a profoundly important role in the relations of indigenous peoples and European newcomers in many of the Anglo-American colonies that would develop. In the Roman Catholic church in general, and in France in particular, the rise of a Protestant challenge provoked both a Counter-Reformation and the emergence of a newly militant spirit of Catholicism. Both Catholic renewal and Catholic militancy were to have profound effects on the Indian peoples of North America.

The upheavals within the ranks of European Christianity stirred renewed desires to take Christ's message to all the world and new vehicles for taking it at precisely the moment France was poised to explore North America. The year of Jacques Cartier's first voyage, 1534, was also the year in which the Spaniard Ignatius Loyola established the Society of Jesus. Just as the Catholic revitalization motivated both clerics and rulers to follow the biblical injunction to evangelize, new missionary organizations emerged to fulfil this aim. The Recollets, a particularly strict branch of the Franciscans, and the Jesuits, an aggressive and militant order, were but two of the many orders that were founded or renewed in the aftermath of the Protestant Reformation. The Jesuits in particular moved eagerly to spread the Christian Word, and by the seventeenth century they were ministering to the Chinese and other Asians. It was the presence of groups such as these missionary orders that was to make the seventeenth century, the period of intensive and concerted efforts to explore and develop Canada, a century of faith. Without this recent evolution in Christianity in Western Europe, the early history of Canada, and the first stages of Indian-European relations, would have been vitally different.

Two Cultures, One Continent

It would have been difficult at any time and in any part of the globe to have found two such different human communities as the Micmac band and Cartier's men who came together at Gaspé in the summer of 1534. The indigenous inhabitants consisted of a multitude of bands and nations of hunter-gatherers and agriculturalists who had adjusted to their environment and lived in harmony with it. They had, especially the agrarian Iroquoians among them, developed elaborate social and political institutions and practices to cope with their large concentrations of population. Their technology and value system made their pressure on the resources of their world light. Lacking iron and firearms, they were unable to inflict much damage on fellow humans and animals; their animistic religion restrained them even from developing the desire to do so. Their economic organization meant that they lived in smaller population concentrations than did Europeans, often faced more threats to their physical well-being, and were forced to coexist with one another and with nature. While they shared a rudimentary form of commerce, similar motives for engaging in warfare, and an essentially similar cosmology and ethics, they had never experienced any need or occasion to combine for economic or political purposes.

The Europeans who came to North America also shared certain characteristics. In Europe, population concentrations were large compared to those in North America; political systems had developed that were authoritarian and coercive rather than communitarian and consensual; and the various economies were increasingly driven by the capitalistic motive of acquisition and investment. European nations also shared a common Christian faith, and, while differences of theological and ecclesiological detail might in the sixteenth century cause them to war with one another, that common faith gave them a similar attitude towards the environment. Their outlook was that of scientifically inclined creatures of God, who were beginning to believe not only that the world was created for their enjoyment but that the rules governing it were knowable and exploitable for economic purposes. Perhaps the different arrangement of the Europeans' mental furniture was the thing that distinguished them most from the indigenous peoples of America.

When Europeans began to undertake voyages to the new world they were setting in train a process that would bring these two contrasting communities out of solitude and into contact. The wonder of it was that early contact between two such different societies should have been so cooperative.

A Young Colony

By Victor Howard

In the following article, Victor Howard, former director of the Canadian Studies Centre at Michigan State University, argues that although there are similarities between the development of Canada and the United States, those wishing to understand Canada will benefit from noticing the crucial differences. He traces the early history of Canada, which like the United States was originally populated by natives who are thought to have arrived on the continent from Asia via the Bering Strait. Following an initial period of settlement by the French, Howard explains, the French succumbed to British power in 1759. In 1774 the British Parliament passed the Quebec Act, which recognized and protected the French presence in Quebec. After the American colonies won their independence, the Canadian part of North America remained British, and in the War of 1812 Canadians and British forces fought together against the United States. Howard concludes by discussing the westward expansion of British North America and its developing relationship to the United States.

Educators and students viewing the history of Canada from the perspective of the United States will find similarities between the development of these neighbors, yet many striking and crucial differences as well. While the two share the experiences of accommodating great numbers of immigrants, a westward expansion, and a democratic political and social ethic, Canada and the United States have lived these experiences in different ways and with different results.

The first human inhabitants of the area now known as Canada migrated in waves from Asia across the Bering Strait and, largely because of the geographical conditions of the areas in which they settled, evolved into numerous distinct tribes. Estimating their number in those centuries of unrecorded history is difficult, and the estimates that exist are often debated and revised as new an-

Victor Howard, "An Introduction to the History of Canada," *Introducing Canada*, edited by William W. Joyce and Richard Beach. Washington, DC: National Council for the Social Studies, 1997. Copyright © 1997 by National Council for the Social Studies. Reproduced by permission.

thropological evidence is discovered. Most sources, however, posit that there were between one and two million Natives in North America above Mexico in the late fifteenth century when Europeans began arriving, and something like 200,000 Natives and Inuit (Eskimo) in the region that was to become Canada. Tribes varied widely from the Kwakiutl (who lived along the Pacific coast, subsisting on salmon, sea and land mammals, and wild fruits, with arts including weaving, basketry, and totem poles) to the Blackfeet (nomads in the mid-continent who hunted buffalo for food, clothing, and tipis and whose culture was characterized by warrior clans, the Sun Dance, and bead and feather artwork) to the Montagnais (nomadic hunters in the semiarctic far north who followed caribou migrations and centered their religious culture on the shaman).

Europeans Arrive

Although Norse sailors found their way to the eastern shores of North America between 1000 and 1400 A.D., the real exploration of that landscape which we now call Canada did not begin until 1497, when John Cabot came ashore onto Newfoundland and Cape Breton Island. In the first quarter of the sixteenth century, these regions were visited by Spanish, Italian, French, Portuguese, and English mariners who fished, stole Indian slaves, charted coastlines and went home to Europe. Jacques Cartier, a Frenchman, ventured up the great river of St. Lawrence in 1535 as far as present-day Montreal. By 1600, all competing interests from Europe had been discouraged, and France could now extend its imperial design onto the continent, calling it "New France."

The first permanent French settlement was established in 1608 at Quebec City by Samuel de Champlain, explorer, cartographer, and agent of the French crown. Champlain brought with him three ambitions: 1) the discovery of a route to China and the East Indies; 2) the development of a fur trade with the aborigines, particularly the beaver pelt so much in demand in Europe; and 3) the conversion of the Indians to Roman Catholicism.

Champlain and his followers soon realized that, by settling along the St. Lawrence Valley, they had at their disposal a remarkable water highway into the interior of the continent. While colonists to the south had struggled across the forests and mountains until they reached the Ohio River, the French thrived along a lake and river system that led directly westward for thousands of miles. And the country to be crossed was rich in furs. The trade was risky and involved regular struggles with the Indians, but it was a profitable enterprise and played a major role in sustaining the French colony for two centuries. Moreover, the search for fur took the French into the Great Lakes Basin and south along the Mississippi River.

Jesuit missionaries arrived not only as priests but as guides, interpreters, explorers, diplomats, and recorders of an extraordinary era. As early as the 1630s, when the Puritans were founding their "City on the Hill" in New England, Father Jean de Brébeuf had already established a large mission among the Hurons far to the north and west.

However successful these initiatives were, the population of New France remained small. By 1670, little more than 8,000 French lived there. A century later, mainly through natural increase rather than immigration, that figure had risen to 70,000, most of whom were *habitants* or farm workers employed on lands owned by an aristocratic class called *seigneurs*. It is from these 70,000 that the several million French Canadians of our time are descended.

French-English Wars

From 1690 to 1759, the French were involved in a series of wars with England and her American colonies as the two powers fought for control of North America. The French believed that the British were moving illegally into the Ohio and Mississippi valleys, where they had no right to be since those regions had first been traveled by French explorers. With Indian allies on both sides, these two European allies attacked and counterattacked along, above, and below the Great Lakes. The flaw in the French enterprise, however, was that nearly all of its supplies, reinforcements, and communications came into the continent through the fortress city of Quebec, overlooking the St. Lawrence River. The British therefore set out to capture Quebec City, which they did in 1759 when an expedition lay siege to the town and its citadel, and, in a final assault, won the day and—for a time—the continent.

In 1774, the British Parliament proclaimed the Quebec Act, which extended the boundaries of New France west and south, recognized the seigneurial system, retained French civil law and the Roman Catholic church, and appointed a legislative council comprised of French and English members directed by a governor. Thus the French presence in Canada was sanctioned by the British and allowed to continue. Nonetheless, New France had become British North America.

In 1782, the British, having lost the American War of Independence, were forced to withdraw from their great empire south of the Great Lakes and the St. Lawrence just as the French had a generation before. The Canada Act of 1791, promulgated by the British government, divided the region it could now claim into two provinces: Upper Canada, now Ontario, and Lower Canada, now Quebec. British North America profited from the arrival of some 40,000 "United Empire Loyalists," refugees who fled the young United States, bearing their loyalty to English rule and law to Canada. These loyalists would thereafter be a prominent element in the population of Canada, in both reality and symbol, a vivid reminder of the historical link with Great Britain.

British North America

Life in Canada in the early nineteenth century was very much a frontier existence: great stretches of sparsely populated terrain; wretched roads; poor postal systems; few schools and churches; and marginal income from farming, lumbering, and fishing. Moreover, the lapsed fashion of beaver hats and capes in Europe ruined that trade. Nonetheless, more settlers arrived from Germany, Ireland, England, Scotland, and from the United States for that matter, to make their homes in Nova Scotia, New Brunswick, and Upper and Lower Canada.

The French and the English, while living side by side, argued constantly and furiously over language priorities, immigration policies, finances, and governmental controls. The War of 1812 briefly thrust these issues into the background as Canadians joined with British military forces in combat against the United States. President James Madison had declared war in a vague effort not only to prevent the British navy from compromising the freedom of the seas but also to extend the concept of Manifest Destiny west and north into the continent. The conflict sprawled along such scattered fronts as Michigan, Niagara, Lake Erie, Lake Ontario, New York, and Washington, D.C. It produced such legends as Laura Secord, a Canadian girl who overheard American officers planning an attack, and who then walked nearly twenty miles to deliver the information to her compatriots. After two years of weary jousting, Britain and the United States accepted the Treaty of Ghent, which effectively restored captured territories to their original owners. The American principle and dream of Manifest Destiny received a severe rebuke.

In the second quarter of the nineteenth century, roads, canals, and railways began to unite the regions; Montreal, Quebec City, and York (later Toronto) grew into active commercial towns; secondary industries such as pulp, flour, and ship construction flourished; several colleges and universities were launched. Most important, perhaps, the quest for "responsible government" gained momentum among English and French alike, particularly during and after the Rebellion of 1837 led by two patriots, William Lyon Mackenzie in Upper Canada and Louis Joseph Papineau in Lower Canada. British rule seemed so autocratic to these two men that they led several hundred other dissenters into the streets, only to be quickly overwhelmed by government troops. But the incident sufficiently alarmed Parliament that it dispatched a senior member of the aristocracy, Lord Durham, to restore order. In his report, however, Durham recommended the union of Upper and Lower Canada and the creation of "responsible government"—i.e., that the Executive Council be made responsible to the Legislative Assembly and not to the Governor. While the Act of Union of 1841 created the United Province of Canada, popular rule was not forthcoming until 1848. That same year, Nova Scotia secured self-determination, with New Brunswick following in 1854, Newfoundland in 1855, and Prince Edward Island in 1862.

Westward Expansion

Meanwhile, Canadians continued to push westward to the Pacific in search of water routes and territory. Two mighty commercial ventures, the Hudson's Bay Company and the North West Company, threw their outposts across the Prairies, into the Rockies, and beyond. Among the recruits to the North West Company was Alexander Mackenzie, the first European to cross the continent. James Frobisher and Simon Fraser gave their names to the waterways they explored. And if the population and authority of the Canadian Pacific coast could scarcely be said to equal that of the Atlantic, it could and did respond when, in the 1840s, the Oregon boundary dispute erupted. The Oregon Territory between California and Alaska had been jointly occupied by American citizens and the English, but when Yankee settlers called for including the area in the United States, James K. Polk, candidate for the American presidency, took as his slogan "54-40 or Fight!" That is, the United States wanted the northern boundary of the Oregon Territory to be set at latitude 54°40' whereas the British wanted it roughly along the 45th parallel. A compromise reached in 1846 set the 49th parallel as the permanent international line between Canada and the United States. In time, this would come to be called the world's longest undefended border.

Tensions continued to ease during the 1850s, once the two nations agreed on a reciprocal trade relationship. Although the agreement was canceled by the United States in 1866, it was evident that trade was inevitable and worthwhile.

Canada's relationship to the United States during the American Civil War was curious. By virtue of their points of contact and associations with northern states, Canadians favored the Union even though Great Britain favored the confederacy. One small band of Southern raiders moved from a Canadian hideout to attack St. Albans, Vermont, the only assault of its kind during the war. On the other hand, thousands of Canadians served with the Union army. And, as we know, the "underground railway" had already taken many escaping slaves into Canada. Their descendants form one of the enduring keystones of the black population of Canada today.

At the end of the Civil War, Canadian leaders faced both new and continuing concerns. They feared that the Americans would again cancel the trade reciprocity agreement, they were anxious about the prospect of American Manifest Destiny, they were concerned about Britain's reluctance to ensure the military defense of its colony, and they had determined the need for a greatly expanded railway system east and west. Consequently, Canadian statesmen led by Georges Etienne Cartier and John A. Macdonald, "the fathers of Confederation," began to forge the means by which nationhood could be secured. The strategy of "Federation" was seized upon as the most appropriate for numerous regions of Canada. A strong central government would still appreciate the need of Canada's regions, soon called "provinces," to have a considerable degree of autonomy.

The American Revolution and the War of 1812

By Barry Gough

Prior to the American Revolution, the North American land mass east of the Mississippi was principally British, with a small but significant French population, known as the Canadiens, *living in and around the area now known as Quebec. In the following selection, Barry Gough, a professor of history at Wilfrid Laurier University in Ontario, discusses the American Revolution and the early, formative relationship between the newly founded United States and the regions to the north. According to Gough, the* Canadiens *resisted joining in the rebellion because they were largely content with their treatment under the British and had some disputes with their Yankee neighbors. During and after the Revolution, Gough reports, the anglophone population of Canada swelled when tens of thousands of Tories, who were loyal to the British, migrated from the United States because of persecution. As Gough sees it, the War of 1812, in which the British and Canadians repulsed American invaders, both strengthened the ties between the British Crown and the fledgling Canada and promoted nationalist sentiment within Canada. For the rest of the nineteenth century, Gough argues, much Canadian policy and development was directed toward countering American power.*

W hy did the *Canadiens* not join the [American] Revolution? For one thing, British military might in the great garrison at Quebec could not be overthrown. For another, the American invasion of 1775 was poorly executed. Finally, the *Canadiens* did not rise against the British, as the Americans had expected. The Quebec Act had not coerced the *Canadiens*; seigneurs, clergy, and habitants [French peasants] had been unmolested since 1763 and preferred the status quo. Though some habitants had helped the invaders from the beginning, many were alienated from "les Yankis" when they received payment for supplies in useless currency or notes. The American general [David] Wooster's decision to prohibit the holding of mass in a Montreal church on Christmas eve, 1775 similarly alienated the *Canadiens*. Quebec and the *Canadiens* had not joined the Revolution. It can be speculated that had Canada been populated by the English for as long as Massachusetts or Virginia, rebellion might have spread and Canada become American. Paradoxically, Canada remained British because its inhabitants were French. . . .

The United Empire Loyalists

The American Revolution induced major migrations to British America, which strengthened pro-empire sentiment while at the same time adding American social and cultural mores to the emerging mosaic north of the border. The Revolution was in many ways a civil war, and the success of the patriot cause in the Thirteen Colonies brought persecution, humiliation, anticonspiracy committees, fines, confiscations, death, test laws, and oaths of allegiance—all designed to make patriots out of Loyalists. As one evacuee put it, "Neither Hell, Hull nor Halifax can afford worse shelter than Boston."

During and after the war, banishment or voluntary exile was the experience of about 100,000 American Tories. Some 40,000, among the first of many displaced persons to find their way to Canada as a result of political upheavals elsewhere, made their way into British North America. About 10,000 of them—of all classes—went to the vacant lands of the St. John River Valley of Nova Scotia. This place and its environs they mockingly called "Nova Scarcity," and this area became a separate colony under the name of New Brunswick in 1784, with its own governor, legislature, and judiciary. Other Loyalists settled in southern Nova Scotia, Cape Breton Island, and Prince Edward Island. Nantucket whalers, more interested in economics than politics, located in Dartmouth, Nova Scotia, to benefit from British mercantile regulations for encouraging the southern whale fishery.

A further 10,000 Loyalists crossed into Canada to settle the Niagara peninsula, the St. Clair River region, and various townships and land grants in what was then southwestern Quebec.

These new colonists, mostly from New York and Vermont, sought an outlet for political liberties they had enjoyed in the American colonies. They wanted their own assembly, separation of their freehold lands from the seigneuries, and complete freehold land tenure. They encouraged relatives and friends to come from the United States and by 1791 there were about 25,000 people living in southern Ontario. By 1812 their number had risen to about 90,000, of whom 20 percent could be classified as "Loyalists," 60 percent as "non-Loyalist Americans" (the "late Loyalists" of various ethnic extractions), and 20 percent as "other." The Loyalists brought slaves with them to Canada but within two decades of the Revolution had begun to equate slavery with the republic they had left, and soon began to end the

AMERICAN GENERAL WILLIAM HULL'S PROCLAMATION TO THE CANADIANS

On July 12, 1812, in the opening days of what came to be known as the War of 1812, American brigadier general William Hull landed at Windsor, a city across the river from Detroit. The next day he issued the following proclamation, which casts the American invaders as liberators of the Canadian people.

Inhabitants of Canada! After thirty years of peace and prosperity, the United States have been driven to arms. The injuries and aggressions, the insults and indignities of Great Britain, have once more left them no alternative but manly resistance or unconditional submission.

The army under my command has invaded your country, and the standard of Union now waves over the territory of Canada. To the peaceable, unoffending inhabitant it brings neither danger nor difficulty. I come to *find* enemies, not to *make* them. I come to protect, not to injure you.

Separated by an immense ocean and an extensive wilderness from Great Britain, you have no participation in her councils, no interest in her conduct. You have felt her

practice and develop movements for abolition. The institution was terminated by statute in Upper Canada in 1793. . . .

The War of 1812

The imperial-colonial relationship and the various British-American colonial identities were further strengthened by war. After the American Revolution, relations between Britain and the United States continued on shaky ground. Some Americans who believed that the only answer was to control Canada repeated statements similar to George Washington's prediction of 1778: "if that country [Canada] is not with us, it will . . . be at least a troublesome if not a dangerous enemy to us."

In addition to the question of security, American politicians

---

tyranny, you have seen her injustice, but I do not ask you to avenge the one or redress the other. The United States are sufficiently powerful to afford you every security consistent with their rights and your expectations. I tender you the invaluable blessings of civil, political and religious liberty, and their necessary result, individual and general prosperity. . . .

In the name of my country, and by the authority of my Government, I promise protection to your persons, property and rights. Remain at your homes, pursue your peaceful and customary avocations, raise not your hands against your brethren. Many of your fathers fought for the freedom and independence which we now enjoy. Being children, therefore, of the same family with us, and heirs to the same heritage, the arrival of an army of friends must be hailed by you with a cordial welcome. You will be emancipated from tyranny and oppression and restored to the dignified station of freemen. Had I any doubt of eventual success I might ask your assistance, but I do not. I come prepared for every contingency. I have a force which will look down all opposition, and that force is but the vanguard of a much greater.

Quoted in *Changing Perspectives in Canadian History*, edited by Kenneth A. MacKirdy, John S. Moir, and Yves F. Zoltvany. Notre Dame, IN: University of Notre Dame Press, 1967, pp. 101–102.

found irritating the commercial ambitions of the empire of the St. Lawrence south of the boundary. Loyalist claims for compensation were not being paid by the United States, and consequently Britain kept control of the southwestern posts until Jay's Treaty of 1794. This agreement ceded the posts to the Americans but allowed Canadian commerce south of the line to continue. The Indians in such areas as the Wabash Valley, who had nothing to say in these matters, tried to keep up the Canadian trade and to resist the encroachment of American settlers. The Battle of Tippecanoe (1811) in which Tecumseh, his brother "The Prophet," and others were to die in the Shawnee cause marked the decline of the Canadian-Indian trading alliance and the rise of American military influence in the Indiana Territory. American politicians then looked for a permanent solution to the interrelated questions of Canadian trade with such tribes as the Shawnee and of land control in the Midwest. The Americans also objected to British treatment of American ships, commerce, and seamen and British political activities in Florida and Texas. The result was that expansionists, both in and out of Congress, sought a military campaign that would strengthen their position in relation to Great Britain. Why not invade Canada, they argued, expel the British from the continent, and make the United States safe, peaceful, and secure?

A Costly Mistake

In deciding to send an army to invade Canada in 1812 the American Congress had underestimated both British power in North America and British determination not to abandon their North American colonies to the Americans. Congress believed, foolishly, that the Ontario peninsula, so heavily populated with American settlers, would be an easy conquest, or, as Thomas Jefferson put it, "a mere matter of marching."

To Canadians and Americans alike, the War of 1812 was a renewal of an old encounter, and most theaters of war were familiar ones—the Atlantic Seaboard, the Great Lakes, and Louisiana. In the Atlantic, despite the early frigate victories that left the American public reeling with success, the British navy acquired command of the sea and by 1813 had enforced a blockade of the coast from Boston to New Orleans. Now the British could press their advantage and in 1813 they gave convoy support to a North West Company expedition to secure the far western fur trade at the mouth of the Columbia, where Americans had been since 1811. The coastal blockade meant that the Americans would have to attack the British at inland points, and they determined to undertake a three-pronged, simultaneous attack on Canada. By the Champlain-Richelieu access, by the Niagara Peninsula, and by Detroit, the American army was to attack and then march on Montreal and Quebec. But the British and Canadians enjoyed a high degree of success on the battlefield. Control of the lakes was sometimes in doubt but never the total control of the Ontario peninsula. The brilliant feats of General Sir Isaac Brock at Queenstown Heights had other parallels along the Canadian border. At the same time, the ill-trained, badly led American forces suffered some embarrassing defeats. Only at New Orleans, where 10,000 British veterans of European campaigns led by Sir Edward Pakenham were repulsed by Andrew Jackson and his frontiersmen in January 1815, did Americans enjoy a splendid victory. Even so, in the irony of circumstances, the battle had occurred fifteen days after the Peace of Ghent had been signed in Belgium.

The war begun for control of North America ended in the maintenance of the *status quo ante bellum*. The Peace failed to resolve the maritime rights question or make a western boundary. But it did allow that a joint commission would resolve several issues including the boundary from the Saint Croix River to the Lake of the Woods, the question of British navigation of the Mississippi, and American rights to fish. Subsequently, the Convention of 1818 provided for a boundary along the 49th parallel from the Lake of the Woods to the Rocky Mountains. The New Brunswick–Maine boundary controversy was not considered, but that of Oregon was discussed and there joint control agreed on. On the fisheries question, the Americans were barred from the in-shore fisheries of the British colonies.

A New View of Canada

Canadians, unlike the Americans, did not view the War of 1812 as an exercise in frustration or an unsuccessful military venture. They regarded it as a great victory for themselves and for the British Empire. More important, the war colored their basic outlook toward the American republic. Loyalists became Canadians. As John Beverley Robinson, the Chief Justice of Upper Canada, claimed, the war "produced in the British colonists a national character and feeling." Robinson and his contemporaries believed that henceforth they would have to fight "a constant struggle for independence against a powerful and unprincipled neighbour." The result was that the Upper Canada Tory governing class employed every means of "state, church, and school to control immigration, check loyalty, ferret out treason, and inculcate the right values." Canadians now began to realize that British North America was not "a kind of subarctic, second-best America, but rather a genuine alternative to this revolution-born democracy, and organized upon principles quite different from it."

Another longstanding effect of the War of 1812 was that both British and United States governments shared a suspicion of the rival's activities in the period 1815 to 1871. Although the Rush-Bagot naval agreement of 1817 limited armed vessels, tonnage, and armaments on the Great Lakes, its provisions were frequently violated by both parties. War clouds gathered during the Oregon boundary controversy in 1844–1846; the San Juan Island dispute, 1859–1860; the United States Civil War, 1861–1865; and the Fenian scares of the 1860s. In British North America the British maintained large garrisons, settled areas for strategic reasons, enlarged militias, and built canals such as the Rideau and Lachine with strategic and commercial considerations in mind. They strengthened forts or naval bases at Montreal, Lake Champlain, Kingston, and elsewhere. They built the huge military stronghold at Quebec after 1823 and expanded the dockyards and citadels at Halifax and Bermuda. On the Pacific coast in the mid-1850s the Royal Navy made its base at Esquimalt, Vancouver Island, in support of British imperial interests. In the Atlantic and Pacific, British squadrons served to counter the rise of American land power. On the other side of the border, Americans took similar military precautions. Clearly, the "undefended border," as some historians in the twentieth century would call it, was mythical. In Canada the prospects of an American military invasion loomed large. They remained so until the last boundary dispute, over Alaska, ended in 1903 and an Anglo-American accord had been reached.

The Achievement of Self-Government

By Gerald S. Graham

According to Gerald S. Graham, a former Rhodes Professor of Imperial History at the University of London, in the early years of the nineteenth century disillusionment over the American Revolution and the mounting costs of maintaining overseas colonies in Canada led many British statesmen to question the imperial system. Furthermore, as Graham explains, the colonists themselves were increasingly dissatisfied with the economic restrictions they believed imperialism imposed. The short-lived Canadian uprising of 1837 forced the British government to confront the colonists' discontent, which it did by approving a move toward responsible self-government. According to Graham, this method of government, in which an elected assembly made decisions on local issues within colonies, represented a major change in the British Empire. It was a chief recommendation of Lord Durham, who in his 1838 report on the state of the colonies also recommended that the provinces of Upper and Lower Canada, which are now Ontario and Quebec, be united under a single government. Durham's vision, Graham recounts, was that the French population be gradually assimilated into an English majority.

In the long-drawn-out reconstruction of the Empire after the American Revolution, British North American problems attracted comparatively little official attention. The unhappy experience with the Thirteen seceding colonies had induced in Britain a mood of irritated disillusionment with white colonies of settlement, a feeling that was indirectly intensified as a result of growing interest in the commercial potentialities of the Far East. The Old Colonial System had been intended to secure for Great Britain not only the sole exploitation of British North American resources, but full control over colonial import and export trade. Unhappily, this grandiose ideal of a self-sufficient empire—never

Gerald S. Graham, *Canada: A Short History*. London: Hutchinson's University Library, 1950. Copyright © 1950 by Hutchinson's University Library. Reproduced by permission.

more than partially attained—had been broken by a successful colonial revolt, and any efforts to redeem it seemed hopeless.

It was natural, therefore, that many statesmen should be sceptical of further colonial projects and expenditures. Angry and disillusioned they cursed the costs of empire. Only a scant few zealots, in an effort to stem the tide of economy and calumny, tried to right the balance, and portray within the wilderness of the new world 'an inexhaustible mine of wealth' waiting the endeavours of an impatient and short-sighted mother country. Sir Guy Carleton, with unequalled prestige and authority in the field of colonial affairs, had solemnly asserted that the Maritimes and Canada would be fully capable within a few years of supplying the West Indies with all the food and lumber they required. His glowing panoramas impressed colonial officials, who for a fleeting moment were able to visualize a colonial granary, a vast reserve of naval stores and timber, and a potential market for British manufactures and West India sugar and rum.

As events turned out, however, these provinces continued to have great difficulty in meeting their own bare needs. . . .

The Expense of Colonies

In all probability the British North American colonies *were* economic luxuries, although it is well to realize that no attempt at accurately estimating their cost had ever been made. No direct accounts were laid before parliament, and no one had ever added up the different items of expense—ordnance, commissariat and naval accounts—apart from the costs of civil and military expenditure within the colonies themselves. It was simply taken for granted that the mother country was paying through the nose for very little in return. According to the reckoning of the *Edinburgh Review*, the Canadas [Upper and Lower Canada, now Ontario and Quebec] alone before 1815 had drained the country of between sixty and seventy millions, of which probably half a million a year went 'for the mischievous patronage of appointing its governors, generals and judges'.

None the less, despite these costly attentions, there was a growing uneasiness in British North America about the whole method and spirit of British colonial practice. Had the Trade and Navigation laws been enforced in their original vigour, the Maritime Provinces, for example, would probably have increased their trade with the West Indies. But as things were, the admission of

American shipping had given to the southern and middle States a complete monopoly of the West Indian provisions and lumber traffic without offering any countervailing advantage to the British colonies in the north. The United States had managed to penetrate the British colonial system, but the British colonies had no authority to seek or to demand reciprocal treatment in American markets, and were in fact on numerous occasions paying the penalty of their colonial status.

A Call for Change

'It is immediately necessary,' declared a Joint Committee of the Assembly and Council of Nova Scotia in 1818, 'that the colonies, in addition to the privileges they now enjoy, should be allowed the same freedom with all the world which the people of the United States have acquired.' 'What does British North America offer to immigrants?' was the question posed by a shrewd critic of Nova Scotian affairs, Richard John Uniacke. 'Nothing but a temporary refuge in a number of disunited and ill-organized Colonies, the commercial interests of which are regulated by a code of Laws, framed during the influence of a miserable and contracted policy, such as could view with jealousy the manufacture even of a nail or a hat in a Colony'. . . .

Many radicals were willing, it is true, to cut all restrictions, commercial as well as political, and risk the chance of colonial desertion; but most liberal Whigs [one of the British political parties] such as Lord Durham were not yet prepared to remove all the bonds even in a world of free trade. Trustful of colonial loyalty, they stuck to their belief in an enduring centralized Empire, and by their attacks on bureaucracy and constant agitation of imperial issues they forced ministers to defend themselves and declare their policy. It was fortunate for the Empire, at the moment when the reckless leader of the Reform group in Upper Canada, William Lyon Mackenzie, was gathering his rebel force near Toronto preparatory to overthrowing the government by force, that a group of British liberals should have been mulling over a solution to the colonial dilemma which was to face the British government so urgently in 1838.

Violence Breaks Out

The uprising of 1837 in the Canadas, although portentous in its consequences, was not a real rebellion. Only a bare handful took

part in it, and in neither province did it reach dangerous pro-
portions, although it did encourage border filibustering and in
that sense might have precipitated war with the United States.
In Upper Canada it would never have broken out had not the
lieutenant-governor, Sir Francis Bond Head, purposely with-
drawn his troops from the scene of trouble in order that the dis-
sident elements should play into his hands. In Lower Canada it
was the work of a few extreme radicals, and in no sense represented militant French nationalism. Thanks to the Quebec Act,
the Roman Catholic Church refused from the beginning to support the insurgents, and the attitude of the clergy made failure
inevitable.

But the so-called Rebellion had at least the merit of forcing
the British government to face the issue of whether or not the
will of the colonial people should be the deciding element in local government. Discontent was rife in all the provinces; reform
was not simply a Canadian issue [that is, an issue in Upper Canada
and Lower Canada]. The movement for increased self-government
was just as vigorous in Nova Scotia and New Brunswick, although
men like Joseph Howe and Lemuel Wilmot sought their ends by
constitutional means. That the problem was wide in its imperial
significance is indicated by the title and powers of the man who
was given the thankless task of trying to solve it. Lord Durham
was not only given a special commission for enquiring into the
causes of Canadian discontent, he was also made Governor-in-
Chief of the Provinces of Upper Canada, Lower Canada, New
Brunswick, Nova Scotia and Prince Edward Island.

Durham arrived at Quebec in May of 1838 and his famous
Report was completed in the following February, hardly more
than a year before his death. It was an inauspicious moment to
talk about the mother country's obligations to the Empire. While
economists piled up expense accounts showing the staggering
costs of maintaining colonies, indiscreet politicians were beginning to talk about the coming blessing of colonial independence.
Amid this depressing scene, the Durham Report came as a star-
tling challenge.

The Reform of Government

Like the great [Lord] Chatham, Durham recalled his country to
a sense of her responsibilities, but unlike Chatham, he demanded that the Empire should advance on a new basis of self-

government for individual parts. Local interests, he declared, were obviously as important to the colonists as imperial interests were to the mother country, and it was futile and absurd to ask advice on matters of purely domestic concern from a government some 3000 miles across the sea. Hence, to break the deadlock between executive and people, he recommended what was perhaps the obvious concession, namely, that the executive council or cabinet must be made responsible to the majority of the elected assembly in every matter relating to local affairs. Foreign affairs, the constitution of government, external trade and commerce and the disposal of Crown lands were excluded.

The second major feature of his Report was the union of the Canadas under a single government; Durham had brilliantly conceived the idea of a Canadian nation, possessing a recognized status vis-à-vis the United States. Yet here we come to the vulnerable and inconsistent part of his analysis. Despite his advanced, if not radically liberal approach to constitutional problems, Durham in his effort to create a nation was prepared to destroy the French as a racial and cultural minority. Like Chatham's imperialism, his own allowed for no diversity of nationality; and he feared, moreover, the consequences of giving control of the executive to a provincial legislature which should consist almost entirely of poorly educated French Canadians. 'In any plan,' he wrote, 'which may be adopted for the future management of Lower Canada, the first object ought to be that of making it an English province; and that, with this end in view, the ascendancy should never again be placed in any hands but those of an English population'. He proposed, therefore, that the two provinces should be united to swamp the French, and he counted on increased British immigration to maintain the balance until the French population should be thoroughly assimilated.

To sensitive French-Canadians, it is understandable that Lord Durham should appear as an enemy of their country, '*un prophète de malheur*' [prophet of misfortune], and that his allusions to the assimilated French of Louisiana should seem to be added proof of the voracious purpose of British imperialism. '*Nous ne serons jamais les assimilés de la Louisiane*'. [We will never be assimilated like those in Louisiana] Entirely apart, however, from its lack of sympathy with the French-Canadian point of view, Durham's Report greatly underestimated the tenacity of the *habitant* [French peasant] as well as his fertility. Any plan of extinguishing

French–Canadian language and customs would have been as unworkable as it was unwise.

Nevertheless, this defect in his analysis must not be allowed to
detract from less dramatic recommendations. Chatham and Burke
had talked of liberty as the foundation of imperial rule, but neither had suggested any concrete method of colonial government
that would concede the realities of self-government without risk-
ing the break-up of the Empire. Durham in laying the foundation for a nation within a new British Empire, saw colonial self-
government not as a disruptive charge, but as a cement; like many
of his fellow liberal Whigs he had faith in the cohesive quality of
Anglo-Saxon racial sentiment.

THE HISTORY OF NATIONS

Chapter 2

A Nation
Comes of Age

The Birth of a Nation

BY MICHELLE ATKIN

In the following piece, Michelle Atkin argues that the confederation of 1867, which united Ontario, Quebec, New Brunswick, and Nova Scotia into the Dominion of Canada, was not merely the work of visionary statesmen. Rather, Atkin argues, the Dominion of Canada was born because Britain was concerned about American aggression and thought a confederation would be better able to defend itself. Atkin notes that there was considerable resistance to confederation throughout the colonies, and especially in the Atlantic provinces, which thought they would have little to gain from union and much to lose. Ultimately, however, with the support of Britain and because of talk of annexation in the United States, confederation was achieved. Atkin is a graduate student in library and information studies at McGill University in Montreal.

The dominant interpretation of Canadian history portrays confederation as the achievement of visionary statesmen who "transformed a dream into reality." Another school of thought recognizes the practical and pragmatic impetus for confederation—the internal and external pressures placed on the British colonies in North America that necessitated their working together. Those who subscribe to this second school of thought, such as historian J.C. Bonenfant, believe that confederation was brought about "not by people who desired intensely to live together, but rather by people who could not live separately."

This paper will explore the second school of thought by demonstrating how external pressures compounded internal problems. It will look at confederation as a response to the needs of colonists living in a time of uncertainty and instability. It will also ask the question: to what extent might the British have manipulated the American and Fenian [Irish nationalist] threats to encourage the colonists to work together?

The Rise of the Confederation Movement

Of the external pressures providing an impetus for the confederation movement, the American Civil War struck closest to home. The decline in Anglo-American relations, during the mid-1860s, left the British North American colonies vulnerable. Disregard of neutrality laws and sympathy for the southern states (on whose southern cotton her mills depended) in Britain incited ill will in the United States. Northern extremists viewed a strike against Britain's colonies as justifiable retaliation, and there was some heated talk about annexation.

The actual threat posed by the northern army is debatable. From 1861–1865 it was preoccupied with the Civil War, after which it was exhausted. Public opinion concerning the colonies' vulnerability to attack was reinforced by a new Fenian menace. The Fenian brotherhood, which had come into being in the United States in 1859, posed a threat to colonial security. Fenians hoped to capture the British North American colonies and hold them as ransom in return for the liberation of Ireland. With the end of the American Civil War, the United States northern army was releasing thousands of Irish American soldiers, which would potentially provide manpower for the Fenian cause. This threat was perhaps more psychological than physical. The actions of the Fenians were restricted to a few border skirmishes. However, the combination of the American and Fenian threats, according to Britain, placed the security of British North America in jeopardy.

Britain had neither the resources nor the desire to defend the colonies against such aggression. Creating a federation of British North American colonies offered the means to terminate financial and military support for them. Although Britain had long discouraged the efforts of Canadian politicians to put forward the issue of a federal union for British North America, the government realizing the financial burden of defending the colonies, soon changed its position and decided to encourage unity and independence. [As Robert Jackson and Doreen Jackson note, the British government's] view was simply this: if the colonies were to unite they "would not only be more economically viable and easier to defend, but also, as a self-governing dominion, more responsible for the cost of their own defense." Clearly the British saw in the American Civil War yet another reason for the colonies to take (financial) responsibility for their own defense and internal affairs. Given that the Americans were war weary and that the Fenians were basically a group of unorganized terrorists, Britain, by concentrating on defense as the main issue, was playing on public fears.

The threat of invasion gave politicians in the Province of Canada an incentive to break the political deadlock plaguing their House of Assembly. A constitutional committee was established to work towards ending the deadlock that gripped that province's legislative assembly. The committee reported in favor of a federal system of government for the two sections of Canada, and perhaps, even for all of British North America. Not all politicians were quick to endorse this union, fearing that federation might have the defect of the U.S. constitution—a weak central government. However, politicians such as John A. Macdonald were persuaded to embrace the idea of union on the basis that a larger federation would be stronger and perhaps even pose a potential rival to the United States.

The Anti-Confederation Movement

In an atmosphere of perceived insecurity, confederation offered a sound solution to the pressing problem of the colonies' collective defense. However the decision to enter into a federal union of British North American colonies was not unanimously agreed upon at the time of its proposal. Antoine-Aime Dorion, the leader of the Parti Rouge, feared that the new English majority would overwhelm the French population. Sectionalism, however, was not just an issue between English and French Canadians.

In the Maritimes politicians were initially ambivalent towards the idea of a British North American union. Politicians in Prince Edward Island rejected confederation on several accounts. P.E.I. also feared being overwhelmed by more populous provinces— and felt bloody-minded after the British mishandling of the absentee landlord issue. Where the British Commission (1860) appointed to investigate the situation of absentee landlords had issued a report favoring the islanders, only to have it rejected by the proprietors and the Colonial Office, it was clear that the people of P.E.I. were not about to bend over backwards for the Colonial Office.

A TIME FOR INDEPENDENCE

In 1864, John A. Macdonald, who later became Canada's first prime minister, expressed to a Halifax audience his view that the remaining British colonies in North America were mature enough to stand on their own. The only other option, according to Macdonald, was to become part of the United States.

I am not disposed to insinuate that there is a solitary member of this House who entertains sentiments of disloyalty to Great Britain. We all have a right to express our views, and in fact it is our duty to do so since we are sent here to consider what is best for the interests of Canada *first*; for though we owe allegiance to England, Canada is *our* country, and has the strongest and best claims to our devotion. I, sir, am not one of those Canadians who place the interests of England first, and hold those of Canada in secondary estimation. . . . We ought not to permit ourselves to lose sight of the fact, that with nations as with individuals, the time does arrive when it becomes each person to be responsible for himself, and when he can no longer look to his parents to give him a standing in the world. Sir, the time must come, sooner or later, when this country must cease to be a colony dependent on Great Britain; and whatever we do . . . we ought always to keep the fact plainly before our eyes, that passing events are calling upon us, either to commence the establishment of a nationality for ourselves, or make up our minds to be absorbed in the republic lying along our southern borders. Nothing could be more distasteful to me than to become what is called a citizen of the United States, though I admit the enterprise and intelligence which characterize the people of that country.

Quoted in *Changing Perspectives in Canadian History*, edited by Kenneth A. MacKirdy, John S. Moir, and Yves F. Zoltvany. Notre Dame, IN: University of Notre Dame Press, 1967, pp. 215–16.

Newfoundlanders, like Prince Edward Islanders, also chose not to support confederation. However, [as Douglas Francis, Richard Jones, and Donald Smith argue,] Newfoundlanders "failed to support confederation out of apathy not out of opposition." Confederation did not seem, at the time, to offer Newfoundland any real economic benefits. Canada was simply viewed by many politicians as being too far away. As legislative representative R.J. Pinset put it, "there is little community interest between the Canadas [Upper and Lower Canada, now Ontario and Quebec] and Newfoundland. This is not a continental colony."

New Brunswick opposition arose from questions of financing for the Intercolonial Railway, to the provinces' physical representation in the House of Commons (New Brunswick would only have 15 of the 194 seats). The 1865 election was largely fought over the issue of confederation with the pro-confederation government losing in the end. . . .

Confederation Achieved

By the end of 1865, public support for confederation, [Francis, Jones, and Smith note,] "had all but apparently vanished, except in Canada West." The Atlantic colonies were opposed to a union for British North America and Canada East had serious reservations against it. As sectional concerns undermined public support for Canada, British intervention persuaded the colonial politicians to embrace the concept by focusing on the security issues facing the colonies. . . .

When a pro-confederation delegation arrived in London in 1866, they were welcomed by the mother country; members of the counter anti-confederation delegation, led by Joseph Howe, were not. It was clear whose efforts the British government supported, and Britain did everything in its power to make sure that its Governors in the colonies were supportive of confederation. Additionally, Britain agreed to guarantee the loan interest for the proposed Intercolonial Railway should confederation become a reality, thereby giving the maritimes additional incentive to enter into a union with the Canadas.

The United States was also influential in determining the decision made by the three colonies. Rather than sending its army north to annex the British colonies, the United States moved to terminate the Reciprocity Treaty of 1854. Annexationists argued that the economic hardships resulting from abrogation of the treaty would induce the colonies to seek union with the United States. Ironically, a changing economic tide encouraged the colonies to form a new commercial union among themselves.

The necessary legislation—the British North America Act—received royal assent on March 29, 1867, and came into effect on July 1. Nova Scotia and New Brunswick joined The Province of Canada (divided upon confederation into provinces of Ontario and Quebec), creating the new Dominion of Canada.

Confederation was not directly approved by the people. There were no referendums to determine the public sentiment; the omission of such a referendum was not even deemed significant at the time. Confederation was more the substance of a gentlemanly agreement between a few men united by a noble cause, the preservation of their traditions and the prevention of annexation by the United States. Union provided the solution to the pressing problem of colonial insecurity and instability in the period surrounding the American Civil War. To what extent the British were responsible for manipulating the perceived threat of American aggression is debatable. However it is clear that union worked in Britain's favor. Union effectively transferred (financial) responsibility for defense and internal affairs to the colonies, while enabling Britain to still maintain the prestige of being responsible for the new Dominion's external affairs.

The Race to the West

By Gerald S. Graham

In the following piece, Gerald S. Graham, a former Rhodes Professor of Imperial History at the University of London, outlines the development of Canada from the confederation of 1867 through to the settlement of the West in the first decade of the twentieth century. According to Graham, the Canadian government pushed rapidly forward with a western settlement program because of concerns that aggressive American settlers would occupy and claim the land as theirs. Indeed, Graham argues, much of Canadian policy was in response to official worries over Manifest Destiny, the American aspiration for the whole of the North American continent. Although settlement of the West was slow until around 1900, despite a transcontinental railroad, Graham notes that it boomed after the turn of the century and argues that this period of rapid growth helped foster Canadian nationalism and optimism about the nation's future.

Whatever the motives that governed British actions after the Civil War, the British North America Act which produced the Canadian federation of Ontario, Quebec, Nova Scotia and New Brunswick was a gigantic speculation. Migrations from the United Kingdom after the War of 1812 had helped to fill out the Maritime provinces, but increased prosperity in no way reduced a distinctive regional outlook that was almost national in its expression. Apart from lumber, fish and Cape Breton coal, the Atlantic provinces were not rich in economic resources, and the disparity in wealth and opportunity, as compared with Ontario and Quebec, accentuated the sensitivity that geography had originated. 'We are sold to Canada for the price of a sheep-skin': this was the dismal cry that followed a contrived union, which many regarded as a slick Canadian trick [that is, a trick of the Province of Canada, which after confederation became the provinces of Ontario and Quebec]. As late as 1886, the premier of Nova Scotia won a general election on a platform which called for the repeal of the British North America Act.

In Quebec the racial fears of a minority, which [Deputy Prime Minister] George Cartier had done so much to stem, had not abated. Passionately intent on preserving their separate way of life, the French looked with suspicion on a central government that might tamper with their special privileges. Although the British North America Act had strengthened the guarantees provided by the Quebec Act, safeguarding local control of education, marriage, property and civil rights, the residuum of power lay with the federal authority. Thenceforward, the maintenance and the extension of provincial rights became for Quebec a matter of life and death in the struggle for cultural survival.

Most British Canadians were descendants of immigrants who had come to the country in the nineteenth century, and their attachment to the mother country deeply affected their conception of Canada's role within the British Empire. But French Canadians who had been North Americans for over three hundred years, and whose sentimental ties with France had been abandoned long ago, had no such divided allegiance. In a negative sense, they were supporters of the Empire because Westminster [the British parliament] guaranteed their unique privileges as a minority within the Canadian nation. At the same time, they remained a prickly and highly self-conscious bloc, determined to resist any attempt to strengthen the connection with Great Britain.

Settling the West

Meanwhile, alarmed by the prospect of losing the West to acquisitive American settlers and fur traders, Canadian politicians, supported by British and local railway interests, began to urge the immediate acquisition of the prairies and the extension of the railway system as far as the Pacific coast. Two hundred and fifty thousand square miles of Hudson's Bay Company territory were at stake, 'out of which,' declared Nova Scotia's tribune, Joseph Howe, 'five or six noble provinces may be formed. . . . I am neither a prophet, nor a son of a prophet, yet I believe that many in this room will live to hear the whistle of the steam-engine in the passes of the Rocky Mountains, and to make the journey from Halifax to the Pacific in five or six days.'

In 1860 the Grand Trunk Railway ran only from Sarnia on Lake Huron to Rivière du Loup on the St Lawrence River, 120 miles below Quebec. Three years later, an imaginative reorganization scheme, which had the support of British bankers, contemplated its extension round Lake Superior, south of the Great Shield, to the old Red River colony on the outskirts of present-day Winnipeg; thence, in advance of railhead, the route was to be traced by road and telegraph line to the settlements on the Pacific.

This attenuated project offered but meagre means of transcontinental communication; on the other hand, even the flimsiest physical ties might be important if the West were to be spared engulfment by encroaching swarms of American settlers. From Minnesota alone hundreds of immigrants were wearing a trail to the Red River colony which Lord Selkirk had planted for his Orkney Islanders between 1812 and 1813. Alarmed by the influx, the Hudson's Bay Company found increasing embarrassment in dealing with frontier elements, whose vigorous presence betokened increased American interest and influence.

Across the Rocky Mountains, the situation had been even more critical. Here, as on the prairies, rudimentary administration tottered as trading posts expanded into thriving settlements. A crisis developed quickly when the discovery of gold in the Fraser River started a wild rush of American and other foreign prospectors and gamblers. The immediate intervention of the British government and the creation of British Columbia in 1858 were the result. The next step was the transfer of the Hudson's Bay prairies to the Canadian government in 1869, and with this annexation of the North-West, the way was open for British Columbia to become, albeit with wary reluctance, a province in the Dominion of Canada.

A Railroad to the West

British Columbia accepted the invitation because she was offered unexpectedly generous terms, most tempting of which was the federal government's promise to begin a connecting railway within two years and to finish it within ten. By 1876 the Intercolonial between Halifax and Quebec was complete, but political corruption combined with economic depression slowed building operations to a snail's pace. Not until 1880 did a reorganized Canadian Pacific Railway Company make a belated effort to fulfil the government's pledge. Under the direction of a brilliant American-born engineer, William Van Horne, the plateau of rock and scrub and swamp north of Lake Superior was conquered; then, at headlong speed, the line was pushed across the prairies south of the Saskatchewan Valley as far as Calgary, and finally, in 1883, up fearful gradients, more than five thousand feet above sea-level, through the Kicking Horse Pass; thence through the Selkirks and down the valley of the Fraser River to the Pacific Ocean.

On 7 November 1885 in Eagle Pass, Donald Smith (subsequently Lord Strathcona), one of that great company of Scots Canadian pioneers and builders, drove home the last spike. . . .

At long last [early French explorer Samuel de] Champlain's North-West Passage was a reality; an efficient route to the Far East had been established, and even more significant, a clutter of regional segments was now bound together, however tenuously, into a coast-to-coast national entity.

IMMIGRATION: A HISTORICAL PERSPECTIVE

As the following graph indicates, Canada, like the United States, is a country of immigrants. Immigration peaked in 1913, when just over 400,000 people arrived, fell dramatically during the Second World War, and in recent years has averaged just over 200,000 per year.

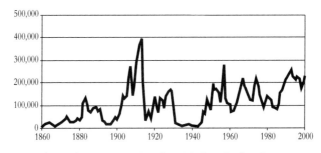

Citizenship and Immigration Canada, original can be found at www.cic.gc.ca.

America's Manifest Destiny

Yet American acceptance of the fact that the North American continent might conceivably be shared between republic and monarchy was an attitude of slow growth. 'I know,' Secretary of State W.H. Seward remarked at the end of the Civil War, 'that Nature designs that this whole continent . . . shall be, sooner or later, within the magic circle of the American Union.' It was expected that tariff pressures alone would gradually build up annexation sentiment. Against such aggressive tactics, Canadians had few resources to throw into the scales, apart from the weight and bargaining power of Great Britain. Moreover, the long list of boundary concessions and surrenders that marked the course of British diplomacy from 1783 to 1871 gave them scant confidence in their champion.

The first Prime Minister of Canada, John A. Macdonald, was sufficient of a statesman and opportunist to realize that British ministers were in no position to push Canadian interests to the limit of war. In terms of Natural Law, Macdonald was right when he exclaimed in a moment of pique that his country had been sacrificed in almost every Anglo-American treaty concerned with British North America. Yet he knew that Canada had much more to lose from a just war than from an unjust treaty. Outraged Canadians might curse the timidity of British appeasers, as they did in 1903 when the terms of the notorious Alaska Boundary award were made public, but Macdonald knew that Canadians, if left to their own resources, had no means of safeguarding the national existence at all. . . .

A New Century

Between 1871 and 1901 a Canadian population of some three and a half millions increased at a rate of probably less than sixty thousand a year. European immigrants were running out almost as rapidly as they had entered. By 1901 more than a million and a half residents of Canada had departed across the border to find a higher standard of living.

But with the opening of the new century, suddenly as by a miracle all was changed. Economic conditions improved rapidly, and likewise self-confidence in a Canadian future. 'The Twentieth Century belongs to Canada': so said Wilfrid Laurier when under his banner the Liberals swept to power in 1896. Twenty-five years earlier, apart from Indians, scarcely more than twelve thousand people lived in the western territories (hitherto owned by the Hudson's Bay Company), and most of these were fur traders. By 1901, with the opening of virgin lands and free homesteads, the population had grown to more than four hundred thousand. During the next decade settlers from eastern Canada, the United States and Europe swarmed into the prairies at the rate of two and three hundred thousand a year, permitting the creation of two new provinces, Alberta and Saskatchewan, in 1905 (Manitoba had been so organized in 1870). By 1911, despite the lethal assaults of hail, grasshoppers, drought and rust, the wide, flat ribbon stretching from Winnipeg to the foothills of the Rocky Mountains contained more than 1,300,000 souls. . . .

Just as the expansion of the American frontier helped to foster an American confidence and cockiness, so did the peopling of the Canadian prairies give stimulus to Canadian imperial impulses. Eastern Canada, the northern United States and the British Isles supplied the vanguard, but the government was soon persuaded to tap the immense labour reservoirs of central and south-east Europe, and under the aegis of the Minister of the Interior, Clifford Sifton, Ruthenians, Poles, Doukhobors and Ukrainians were hurried westward by ship and train. The Ukrainians of Austria-Hungary and Russia were the largest group, and as co-operative farmers, probably the most successful. They brought with them not only stout hearts and skilled hands, but a rich heritage of folk-music, handicrafts, and traditional customs, which the North American melting-pot has fortunately not yet dissolved.

Trade with the Americans

Meanwhile, at the end of the most auspicious decade in Canadian history, the Canadian Prime Minister had finally negotiated what every government had sought since Confederation: a reciprocity trade pact with the United States in the natural produce of farm, forest, river and mine. President Taft was anxious to give the Canadians a good bargain in the hope of extinguishing the last embers of ill-will that boundary disputes and United Empire Loyalist resentments had kept alive. He was eager to establish his country as 'the Good Neighbour'. Unhappily, the agreement encountered much opposition in Congress, and it was only forced through by maladroit use of the argument that a reciprocity treaty was a practical step towards continental union. Such rhetoric was intended for home consumption, but the main impact was felt in Canada. Even without the confusion precipitated in Quebec by Laurier's decision to build a Canadian navy, the threat of Manifest Destiny was sufficient to ensure the defeat of the Liberal government in the general election of 1911. Impelled by a new sense of national kinship, the Canadian people rose in revolt against an arrangement that suggested peaceful annexation. Even the little man was prepared to pay more for his bacon or his bicycle rather than have his country's independence jeopardized.

Not unnaturally, Americans were amazed and perplexed by this unexpected and vigorous outburst of national feeling. It was obviously difficult for them to take Canadian nationhood seriously. Most of the formal official contacts were made through the British Embassy in Washington, and this view of a colonial satellite was confirmed by the ostentatious presence of red pillar-boxes [tall, cylindrical mailboxes], Guards' uniforms, Union Jacks [the flag of the United Kingdom], and the fervent response of Toronto audiences to renderings of the British national anthem. Yet the spawn of European imperialism proved to have an individuality of its own and an almost jingoistic national spirit— anti-American no doubt, but only in the sense that Canadians were determined to preserve a free hand in working out their own destiny. Amid the conflicts of power and diplomacy which had repeatedly tested Anglo-American relations since the War of 1812, a scattered collection of provinces and territories had managed to survive American absorption on the one hand, and any demeaning form of imperial servitude on the other. In the process, a mixed colonial society had achieved, without armed revolution, a separate political identity on the North American continent.

An Equal Among Nations

By B.K. Sandwell

According to B.K. Sandwell, the young nation of Canada took the final steps toward effectively achieving independence through its efforts in the First World War. As Sandwell notes, Canada entered the war automatically when Britain did, and was soon an important source of soldiers, weaponry, and raw materials. So great was the war effort, Sandwell notes, that the government, in the midst of controversy and in the face of resentment in Quebec, had to enact conscription in order to fulfill its obligations. When the war ended, recognition of Canada's sacrifices increased its international profile and earned it a place as a signatory of the Versailles treaty, which concluded the war. Furthermore, according to Sandwell, the 1929 Statute of Westminster granted to Canada and other dominions within the British Empire the status of equal powers in a commonwealth of nations. As Sandwell sees it, by 1941, Canada was effectively independent from Britain except for its membership in the commonwealth and for the fact that it had not been granted, by its own request, the power to amend and interpret its constitution. At the time of writing, Sandwell was the managing editor of Canada's Saturday Night *magazine.*

The outbreak of the First Great War found Canada in a state of considerable economic distress, a circumstance which to some extent facilitated her prompt effective participation; for the enlistment of a volunteer force is easier in a period of wide-spread unemployment. This is not the place to narrate the achievements of the Canadian forces in that tremendous struggle, in which they came in the end to be commanded by a great Canadian officer, General Sir Arthur Currie, a native of Ontario and for many years a resident of British Columbia. The war developed, in the Western Front with which Canada was chiefly concerned, into a prolonged struggle of massive stationary armies, with consumption of munitions on a hitherto undreamed-of scale. So great a proportion of the man-power of Great Britain and France was under arms, and so great a part of Europe's iron-ore deposits was held by the enemy, that Canada was the recipient of immense demands for munitions as well as for fighting men, and by the third year of the war the Government concluded that it would be impossible to keep up the necessary reinforcements for the four Canadian Divisions by voluntary enlistment. At the beginning of 1916 recruiting was bringing in thirty thousand men a month, at the end only six thousand. The Government was losing ground as a result of many administrative weaknesses, some of them inseparable from the conversion of a highly peaceful country into a highly belligerent one; and in various quarters there grew up a demand for conscription and a coalition Government. On May 18, 1917, the day on which the United States Select Draft bill became law, [Conservative prime minister] Sir Robert Borden announced that his Government would introduce "compulsory military service on a selective basis". [Liberal leader of the opposition] Sir Wilfrid Laurier at once decided to oppose such a project. The reasons for his attitude are given by his biographer, O.D. Skelton, as the belief that conscription would not greatly increase the supply of men, and the feeling that Canada was in the war on a different footing from Britain and the United States. These countries "had entered the war as principals"; Canada "had gone in, not for its own sake, but for Britain's". Moreover, "Britain and the United States were not divided historically into distinct and compact racial groups,—except as to Ireland, and no English statesman had attempted to apply compulsion to Ireland,—whereas in Canada this division was the most fundamental and enduring fact in political life". Eleven days later Sir Robert proposed to Sir Wilfrid a coalition Government with equal representation from the two parties, except for his own Prime Ministership, but conditioned on the acceptance of conscription.

Rejecting Conscription

In a letter of June 3, Sir Wilfrid explained to a friend the reasons for his inability to join such a coalition. Reciting the manner in which he had been assailed, and eventually defeated, in Quebec on his own naval proposals, which he had at all times backed with the assurance that "the navy was in no sense a first step towards conscription" and that he was opposed to conscription, he went on: "Now if I were to waver, to hesitate or to flinch, I would simply hand over the province of Quebec to the extremists. I would lose the respect of the people whom I thus addressed". In the [House of] Commons he moved an amendment for a popular referendum on the question, but a large number of English-speaking Liberals voted against him. Under the leadership of Sir Clifford Sifton, and under the pressure of a War Times Election Act which conferred the franchise upon the female next-of-kin of all men in overseas service, disfranchised all citizens naturalized since 1902 whose ancestral language was German, and allowed the ballots of the men overseas to be allotted to whatever constituency the returning officer might see fit (thus making a Liberal victory quite impossible), three federal Liberal ex-cabinet ministers and seven provincial Liberal ministers joined a Union Cabinet, which swept the country in a general election in December 1917. The contest was marked by extreme racial feeling. The war came to an end before it was necessary to admit that the conscription measure was a failure, but it certainly did not provide anything like the number of men anticipated. Dr. Skelton records that out of 404,000 of the first class, unmarried men of 20 to 34, who were registered in 1917, 380,000 claimed exemption; by the end of March 1918, in Ontario 104,000 exemptions had been approved out of 118,000 applied for, and in Quebec 108,000 out of 115,000 applied for. By the end of March only 31,000 had been called up, of whom 5,000 defaulted. At the end of the war 83,000 men had been enrolled under the Act, of whom 22,000 were released on farm leave or compassionate leave. The cancellation of a great many exemptions, chiefly of farm workers, by an Order-in-Council whose legality was maintained only by a four-to-two division in the Supreme Court caused great indignation among the farmers, and was partly responsible for a wave of short-lived farmers' parties and (in the provinces) farmers' governments after 1919. . . .

After the War

The war of 1914–18 effected great changes in the constitutional structure of the British Empire. Canada had put more than 600,000 men under arms, and sent overseas in her own forces some 418,000, not to mention a great number of Canadians who served brilliantly in Imperial forces and especially in the British air forces. She had 60,000 dead and 218,000 casualties. Her men held their ground against the first gas attack of the war, in April 1915, and in 1917 had attached the name of Canada imperishably to the soil of Vimy Ridge.

One of the results of these achievements was a great increase in the autonomy of the Dominion. Sir Robert Borden, though he acted during the war as a member of the Imperial War Cabinet, emerged from the war period with a profound conviction that, in the words of the historian, George M. Wrong, "Canada must not be drawn into any centralized union. Relations with Great Britain must be based on Canada's equality with her as a nation, co-operating freely as occasion might arise, but always as opinion in Canada might decide". He therefore insisted on Canada's separate signature on the Treaty of Versailles [which ended World War I] and on separate membership in the League of Nations for each self-governing Dominion. The situation thus created was formally recognized and defined in 1926 by a Declaration of the Imperial Conference, and was registered in law five years later as the Statute of Westminster. This Statute declares that "the Crown is the symbol of the free association of the members of the British Commonwealth of Nations, and as they are united by a common allegiance to the Crown" the assent of all of them should be necessary to any alteration in the law touching the Succession to the Throne or the Royal Style and Titles. It prohibits the extension of any United Kingdom law to any Dominion "as part of the law of that Dominion" without its consent; and it confers full legislative power on the Dominions, including the power to make laws with extra-territorial operation. By an express exception, the Statute does not apply to the constitution of Canada (the British North America Act), which remains unamendable except by the British Parliament. As already noted, the British Parliament acts automatically to carry out the petition of the Canadian Parliament in this matter; but what it would do if the petition of Canada were opposed by a counter-petition from Quebec or British Columbia, for example, is somewhat uncertain. It has already refused to receive a petition from an Australian State for separation from the Australian Commonwealth; but that is not a parallel case, for the Commonwealth constitution expressly makes Australia responsible for its own constitution, while the Canadian constitution leaves the responsibility with the British Parliament, and the Statute of Westminster expressly preserves that arrangement.

The Second World War

The other important power of complete nationhood, the power to declare war, remained in some doubt until 1939, when the neutrality of Eire [Ireland] (whose position is that of "Dominion Status"), and the entry of Canada into the war by resolution of Parliament several days after the declaration by Britain, seem to have put the answer beyond doubt. It had long been admitted that Canada could not be compelled to fight by any action of the British Government, but many authorities had maintained that she became technically in a state of war as soon as Britain declared war. That theory is now disposed of.

Since the King cannot be personally present in all his Dominions at once, the functions of the Crown are performed for Canada by a Governor-General. In matters within the competence of the Dominion Parliament he can act, and for many years has acted, only on the advice of Ministers who possess the confidence of the House of Commons. So long as the competence of the Dominion Parliament was limited, he was, as regards matters outside of that competence, an official of the British Government, acting under its instructions. The Imperial Conference of 1926 declared that he was to hold "the same position in relation to the administration of public affairs in the Dominion" as the King holds in Great Britain, and was not the representative or agent of the British Government or any Department of it.

A Unique Form of Independence

Canada is now, therefore, a completely independent nation except for three points. The first of these, common to the other Dominions, is whatever constitutional relation is implied by a "common allegiance" with the United Kingdom and the other Dominions to the Crown—and that "common allegiance" does not at present include any necessary common action in war and peace. The other exceptions, the power to amend the constitution, and the power to interpret the constitution, are special to Canada. These powers remain with Great Britain by Canada's desire, for the time being; but the fear of French-Canadians that Canada would be less scrupulous about their ancient rights than Great Britain is rapidly diminishing. In the words of Professor Wrong, "the fear is probably groundless; the French are too powerful for any government to tamper with their guaranteed rights".

The Constitution Comes Home

By Pierre Elliott Trudeau

It was not until 1982 that Canada acquired the power to amend its own constitution, severing its last dependent tie with Britain. As Prime Minister Pierre Elliott Trudeau explains in his speech at a ceremony marking the occasion, when Canada effectively became an independent country some fifty years earlier, it asked Britain to retain the power to amend the constitution because the federal and provincial governments could not agree on an amending formula. In his speech, which is reprinted below, Trudeau also discusses the Charter of Rights and Freedoms, part of the 1982 Constitution Act, which guarantees certain rights and freedoms for all Canadians. According to Trudeau, the Charter strengthens the rights of the French and other minorities in Canada, and entrenches what are known in Canada as transfer payments, through which richer provinces help support less affluent provinces.

Today [April 17, 1982], at long last, Canada is acquiring full and complete national sovereignty. The Constitution of Canada has come home. The most fundamental law of the land will now be capable of being amended in Canada, without any further recourse to the Parliament of the United Kingdom.

In the name of all Canadians, may I say how pleased and honoured we are that Your Majesty and Your Royal Highness have journeyed to Canada to share with us this day of historic achievement.

For more than half a century, Canadians have resembled young adults who leave home to build a life of their own, but are not quite confident enough to take along all their belongings. We became an independent country for all practical purposes in 1931, with the passage of the Statute of Westminster. But by our

Pierre Elliott Trudeau, "Remarks by the Prime Minister at the Proclamation Ceremony on April 17, 1982," www.nlc-bnc.ca, April 17, 1982.

own choice, because of our inability to agree upon an amending formula at that time, we told the British Parliament that we were not ready to break this last colonial link.

After fifty years of discussion we have finally decided to retrieve what is properly ours. It is with happy hearts, and with gratitude for the patience displayed by Great Britain, that we are preparing to acquire today our complete national sovereignty. It is my deepest hope that Canada will match its new legal maturity with that degree of political maturity which will allow us all to make a total commitment to the Canadian ideal.

I speak of a Canada where men and women of aboriginal ancestry, of French and British heritage, of the diverse cultures of the world, demonstrate the will to share this land in peace, in justice, and with mutual respect. I speak of a Canada which is proud of, and strengthened by its essential bilingual destiny, a Canada whose people believe in sharing and in mutual support, and not in building regional barriers.

I speak of a country where every person is free to fulfill himself or herself to the utmost, unhindered by the arbitrary actions of governments.

An Act of Defiance

The Canadian ideal which we have tried to live, with varying degrees of success and failure for a hundred years, is really an act of defiance against the history of mankind. Had this country been founded upon a less noble vision, or had our forefathers surrendered to the difficulties of building this nation, Canada would have been torn apart long ago. It should not surprise us, therefore, that even now we sometimes feel the pull of those old reflexes of mutual fear and distrust.

Fear of becoming vulnerable by opening one's arms to other Canadians who speak a different language or live in a different culture.

Fear of becoming poorer by agreeing to share one's resources and wealth with fellow citizens living in regions less favoured by nature.

The Canada we are building lies beyond the horizon of such fears. Yet it is not, for all that, an unreal country, forgetful of the hearts of men and women. We know that justice and generosity can flourish only in an atmosphere of trust.

For if individuals and minorities do not feel protected against the possibility of the tyranny of the majority, if French-speaking Canadians or native peoples or new Canadians do not feel they will be treated with justice, it is useless to ask them to open their hearts and minds to their fellow Canadians.

Similarly, if provinces feel that their sovereign rights are not secure in those fields in which they have full constitutional jurisdiction, it is useless to preach to them about cooperation and sharing.

The Constitution which is being proclaimed today goes a long way toward removing the reasons for the fears of which I have spoken.

We now have a Charter which defines the kind of country in which we wish to live, and guarantees the basic rights and freedoms which each of us shall enjoy as a citizen of Canada.

It reinforces the protection offered to French-speaking Canadians outside Quebec, and to English-speaking Canadians in Quebec. It recognizes our multicultural character. It upholds the equality of women, and the rights of disabled persons.

The Constitution confirms the longstanding division of powers among governments in Canada, and even strengthens provincial jurisdiction over natural resources and property rights. It entrenches the principle of equalization, thus helping less wealthy provinces to discharge their obligations without excessive taxation. It offers a way to meet the legitimate demands of our native peoples. And, of course, by its amending formula, it now permits us to complete the task of constitutional renewal in Canada.

A Divided Quebec

The government of Quebec decided that it wasn't enough. It decided not to participate in this ceremony, celebrating Canada's full independence. I know that many Quebecers feel themselves pulled in two directions by that decision. But one need look only at the results of the referendum in May, 1980, [in which Quebec voted 60 percent to 40 percent not to separate from Canada] to realize how strong is the attachment to Canada among the people of Quebec. By definition, the silent majority does not make a lot of noise; it is content to make history.

History will show, however, that in the guarantees written into the Charter of Rights and Freedoms, and in the amending formula—which allows Quebec to opt out of any constitutional arrangement which touches upon language and culture, with full financial compensation—nothing essential to the originality of Quebec has been sacrificed.

Moreover, the process of constitutional reform has not come to an end. The two orders of government have made a formal pledge to define more precisely the rights of native peoples. At the same time, they must work together to strengthen the Charter of Rights, including language rights in the various provinces. Finally, they must try to work out a better division of powers among governments.

It must however be recognized that no Constitution, no Charter of Rights and Freedoms, no sharing of powers can be a substitute for the willingness to share the risks and grandeur of the Canadian adventure. Without that collective act of the will, our Constitution would be a dead letter, and our country would wither away.

It is true that our will to live together has sometimes appeared to be in deep hibernation; but it is there nevertheless, alive and tenacious, in the hearts of Canadians of every province and territory. I wish simply that the bringing home of our Constitution marks the end of a long winter, the breaking up of the ice-jams and the beginning of a new spring.

For what we are celebrating today is not so much the completion of our task, but the renewal of our hope—not so much an ending, but a fresh beginning.

Let us celebrate the renewal and patriation of our Constitution; but let us put our faith, first and foremost, in the people of Canada who will breathe life into it.

It is in that spirit of faith, and of confidence, that I join with Canadians everywhere in sharing this day of national achievement. It is in their name, Your Majesty, that I now invite you, the Queen of Canada, to give solemn proclamation to our new Constitution.

Two Solitudes: The French and the English

French Canada to 1900

BY RICHARD BEACH AND MARTIN LUBIN

In the following article, Richard Beach and Martin Lubin discuss the early French presence in what is now Canada. They note that French explorers were the first Europeans to seriously investigate the northern part of the continent, but that the British, who were more active in settling and developing the continent, quickly overcame this early lead. The 1763 Treaty of Paris, which ended years of armed conflict between Britain and France, granted Britain almost total control over the eastern part of North America. Beach and Lubin trace the development of the French-speaking population over the next hundred and fifty years, arguing that it was able to survive because of the protection afforded by the 1774 Quebec Act and an extraordinarily high birthrate. They also focus on the Métis, the francophone, Roman Catholic descendants of French explorers and Native Americans, and their conflict with English-speaking Canada. Beach is director of the Center for the Study of Canada at the State University of New York at Plattsburgh, and Lubin is an associate professor of political science at that university.

Notwithstanding John Cabot's English-supported voyages along the coast of Newfoundland during the 1490s, the French sponsored the first serious attempts to explore and claim for France what is presently Canada. French fishing fleets first plied the coastline around the turn of the 16th century. The Italian Verrazano, under the French flag, explored and mapped sections of the eastern archipelago during the 1520s. Several years later French adventurer Jacques Cartier, with the support of King Francis I, explored the coastline and became the first European to penetrate the heart of the continent in search of gold and a route to the Orient.

In 1534, during the first of his three voyages, Cartier explored the Gulf of St. Lawrence and established contact with the native peoples along the Gaspé Peninsula. He returned to France the same year full of enthusiasm and imaginative Indian tales of the exotic "Kingdom of the Saguenay" in the interior. The next year, he skirted the islands of Newfoundland, Cape Breton, Prince Edward and Anticosti, and again explored the Gulf of St. Lawrence. Most important, he traveled up the St. Lawrence River as far as the rapids near the Island of Montreal. The expedition, however, was fraught with disaster. Cartier and his fearless adventurers decided to winter near the Indian village of Stadacona (Quebec City). The men were ill-equipped to cope with the rigors of the "Canadian" environment and many died of starvation and disease. Cartier and the survivors returned to France the next spring with no concrete evidence of wealth or knowledge of the illusory kingdom.

Undaunted, he was successful six years later in persuading the authorities to attempt another voyage. No route to the Orient was found, the native population was far less friendly, having been ill-treated and exploited by Cartier previously, and little wealth other than exotic flora and fauna was discovered. The failure of these expeditions coupled with important preoccupations in Europe resulted in the French government abandoning for nearly 75 years any further attempts at exploration or settlement in the New World. Whatever early advantage the French, in competition with their European rivals, could have had to establish a permanent foothold, and a claim to the continent, therefore, was lost.

The Father of French Canada

During the French hiatus, explorers, traders and fishermen, as individuals or representatives of other European governments and commercial interests, explored the coastline of North America from Florida to Labrador. The novelty of their adventures stirred the imaginations (and bank accounts) of entrepreneurs, but little of value was found except an abundance of fish. Although individual Frenchmen probably continued fishing and trading with the Indians during the late 1500s, not until 1603 with the arrival of soldier-geographer and "Father of French Canada," Samuel de Champlain, did the French make a renewed effort to explore and to settle Canada. Thereafter, a French presence and influence in North America became firmly established.

Champlain and his partner de Monts attempted a settlement on an island in the St. Croix River, now the Maine–New Brunswick border. Although this first effort was a failure, two years later a far more suitable site was chosen in the Annapolis Valley in what is now the Province of Nova Scotia. Port Royal, as the little fortress was called, subsequently became the center of Acadia, France's first permanent colony in Canada.

Furs, especially beaver, had superseded fish as the motive of most commercial ventures in northern North America. Aware that this resource was far more plentiful in the interior, Champlain in 1608 retraced Cartier's steps up the St. Lawrence in search of a location for a French settlement nearer the heart of the beaver's domain. The site he chose lay below the cliffs of Quebec City. For several decades *L'Abitation* served as the center of the French commercial and political empire in North America.

The growth of the colonies in Acadia and along the St. Lawrence was extremely slow during the 17th and 18th centuries. The support of French authorities was for the most part half-hearted or indifferent. Geopolitical preoccupations in Europe and the attraction of greater wealth and resources elsewhere in the French colonial empire precluded much interest in expanding and subsequently consolidating and protecting the dispersed and underpopulated North American colonies. Few people were willing to emigrate from France to these fledgling colonies. Especially unattractive to potential settlers were the inhospitable climate and physical environment, the terror of Indian warfare and raids, and a quasi-feudal system of land tenure based on large tracts of land known as *seigneuries*.

Moreover, economic structures established by the French government did not encourage expansive settlement. The economy and land settlement policy of Nouvelle France remained inextricably linked to the fur trade and was, until at least the 1660s, rigidly monopolistic. Indeed, the fur trade by its very nature often precluded the establishment of a settled and orderly way of life in the colony. Expansion of the fur trading web, without either parallel expansion of economic and political infrastructures or immigration from France, merely weakened the already tenuous hold that French military and religious leaders had upon the lives and lands under their jurisdiction.

A Bold Expansion

Throughout the 17th century, however, the indomitable and legendary *coureurs de bois*—French explorers like LaVérendrye and de la Salle—and courageous Roman Catholic missionaries—like Joliet and Marquette—crisscrossed more than half the continent, exploring, mapping the land, and spreading Christianity among the native people. By the end of the 17th century, the French empire stretched in a huge arc from the Gulf of St. Lawrence, through the entire region of the Great Lakes to the Rockies, into the Ohio Valley, and down the Mississippi to the Gulf of Mexico. Except for the colonies in Acadia and along the St. Lawrence, however, where permanent settlements were rooted, only a scattered system of forts and fur trading posts existed to maintain French control over the millions of square miles of territory.

The French empire in North America had reached its apogee by the turn of the 18th century and signs of the inevitable collapse appeared soon after. As early as the 1670s, an encirclement began as the British established footholds in Hudson Bay to the north and along the coasts of Newfoundland and Nova Scotia to the east. Most significantly, the string of French outposts in the "West" presented a hindrance and a menace to the increasingly expansionist-minded English (American) colonies to the south.

Reflecting French military and diplomatic failures in Europe, rather than significant military defeats in the New World, the Treaty of Utrecht, signed by the French and the British in 1713, nevertheless signaled the disintegration of the French empire in North America. The Hudson Bay region, Newfoundland and French Acadia were ceded to the British, leaving only Ile St. Jean (Prince Edward Island) and Ile Royale (Cape Breton Island), with the formidable fortress of Louisbourg, to guard the St. Lawrence colony. These changes effectively reduced the threat of French raids along the coast and protected the English fishing fleets. For the next 40 years, the struggle between the British and French intensified, with economic and political control of the North American continent the prize.

Victory for the British

The final chapter in the long-festering conflict between the two European rivals was written in the 1750s. The odds against French success were overwhelming. The population of the English colonies by then was nearly 2 million, while the French numbered fewer than 80,000. Moreover, France had become increasingly involved in European wars and virtually left the people of Nouvelle France to fend for themselves. British probings along the east coast increased and the Iroquois, long the scourge of the French colonies, harassed the dispersed and un-dermanned French outposts.

Owing to British inexperience in the ways of wilderness war-fare, the French initially repelled the attacks and even had some successes. The British inevitably gained the upper hand. With their superior fleet and arms, they captured Louisbourg in 1758, leav-ing the entire French colony along the St. Lawrence vulnerable to attack. The next year, General Wolfe defeated the French at Que-bec City in one of the most important battles ever fought on the North American continent. Within months, Three Rivers and Montreal surrendered. The Treaty of Paris, signed in 1763, ceded the entire French empire in Canada to the British, except for two small islands in the Gulf of St. Lawrence. Most of the French no-bility and some of the bourgeoisie returned to France, leaving 60,000 peasants, *les habitants* [French peasant farmers], and some lower echelon clergy to fend for themselves under British rule.

French Canada in the latter half of the 18th century was com-prised of the little colony along the St. Lawrence and pockets of Acadians located throughout what were to become the Maritime Provinces. Surprisingly, these conservative, Catholic, land-based French-speaking people survived, even flourished, under the con-trol of their aggressive, entrepreneurial, Protestant, and English-speaking masters.

Rights for the French

Several events ensured their survival. In 1774 the British govern-ment passed the Quebec Act, giving the French the right to their language, religion and certain civil laws. This major concession to the population of "Quebec" was a de jure, but not yet de facto, acceptance and recognition of a French-speaking province within the British Empire. There was, of course, a very pragmatic and strategic rationale for the passage of this Act—to placate the French and at least neutralize them should revolt occur in the re-fractory "American" colonies to the south. Despite the appar-ently magnanimous tenor of the Quebec Act, the British fully expected that with an infusion of British settlers and, after 1780, "Loyalist" refugees and immigrants from the United States, the French-speaking population would eventually be assimilated. They were wrong. Isolated from the mother country, and eco-nomically and culturally alienated from the British and Americans, but with the guarantee of their fundamental rights, the French Canadian population during the last decades of the 18th century turned inward, remaining almost oblivious to the English political and commercial environment around them. They depended more heavily than ever upon the church for leadership and inspiration. Especially in the Quebec colony, the lusty indigenous population grew rapidly as a result of an extraordinarily high birthrate and relatively low death rate. By the turn of the century, the survival of the French-speaking population was virtually assured; some segments of the bourgeoisie and clerical elites even sought accommodation with the English leaders.

Yet the British were never comfortable with this rapidly expanding, though basically passive, population in their midst. Several ill-founded and unsuccessful efforts were made to assimilate or at least to suppress French attempts to obtain political influence. The Constitutional Act of 1791, for example, subdivided the large Quebec colony into two parts—Upper Canada, the territory surrounding the Great Lakes (which subsequently became the Province of Ontario), and Lower Canada (the seigneurial land straddling the St. Lawrence and Richlieu Rivers (later to become the Province of Quebec). The minority English population in the old Quebec colony, most of whom had settled west of Montreal, thus avoided potential domination by the more numerous French Canadians living in the St. Lawrence Lowland. The Act also attempted to provide suitable political institutions for both the English- and French-speaking populations.

This new political system lasted less than 50 years. By the 1830s, the populations of the two Canadas had matured and could no longer be kept in the straight jacket designed for them in 1791. Resistance to the authority and elitism of the British and indigenous oligarchs led to rebellions in both Canadas. Each was quickly suppressed, leaving distrust and fear of the English for many years among the French in Lower Canada.

The British soon sent the Earl of Durham to assess the situation and prescribe remedies for the management of the obstreperous colonies. His report, completed in 1839, is one of the most important documents in Canadian history. He was sympathetic to the complaints of both the French- and English-speaking populace, but implicit in the report was the suggestion that the French population in Lower Canada be assimilated by the English. One important recommendation, soon effectuated, was the reunification of Upper and Lower Canada to form again a "Canadian" colony.

A Booming Population

The period of the 1830s was a social watershed for the French Canadian population of Lower Canada. The high birthrate soon exceeded the carrying capacity of the St. Lawrence Lowland and resulted in a massive outmigration of people. What began as a trickle in the 1830s, became a flow in the 1840s and a flood in the 1850s; this emigration lasted for decades thereafter.

Many unskilled rural folk were lured to the towns and cities, especially Quebec City and Montreal, thus reducing significantly the proportion of the English population in urban areas. Aided by church leaders who hoped to avoid the trend toward urbanization, which they perceived as corrupting and degrading, huge tracts of marginal land north of the St. Lawrence Valley and in the Lake St. John region were opened up for settlement. The population spilled into the Ottawa Valley, eastern Ontario, and south of Montreal. Attracted especially by jobs in the textile factories, countless thousands moved southward to the border areas and to towns in the northern United States. In New England they added an entirely new ethnic element to many staid towns and villages. Others sought their fortunes on the western frontier in both Canada and the United States. By the 1860s, the French Canadian population, while still heavily concentrated in the St. Lawrence Lowland, had become much more geographically dispersed.

The new political system in the "Canadian" colony during this time had become virtually unworkable. Thanks in part to the events in the United States, a solution was found or—as some would stress—forced upon the colonies. Faced with increased British indifference or exasperation with their colonies in North America and the considerable threat from the still expansionist-minded United States, the leaders during the early 1860s sought a political system that would provide a stronger united front against the U.S. After several years of negotiations, it was agreed that a quasi-federal system should be formed, in many aspects independent of Great Britain. French Canadian leaders in particular agreed to the plan on the condition that the Canadian colony once again be divided to create a political entity for the French Canadian population in the St. Lawrence Valley and environs. With the passage of the British North America Act on July 1, 1867, by a somewhat relieved British Parliament, the new provinces of Ontario and Quebec, a rather hesitant Nova Scotia and New Brunswick joined to form the Dominion of Canada.

One of the first actions of the new Canadian government was to purchase Rupert's Land, in what is now northern Canada, from the Hudson's Bay Company and eventually give portions of it to Ontario and Quebec. The provinces of Quebec and Ontario were enlarged many times as a result.

Beyond Quebec

From the time of the first settlements, there has never been a contiguous French Canada. This fact was even more evident during the latter half of the 19th century. French Canada by 1870 had expanded considerably from its colonial cores along the St. Lawrence and Annapolis Valleys. While the new Province of Quebec remained indisputably the heartland, other distinctive and distinguishable French Canadian areas had developed primarily as the result of migrations from Quebec to adjacent regions of Ontario and to northern and southwestern sections of that province. A new Acadian heartland had developed and expanded in northern New Brunswick. Acadian areas were also located in southern Nova Scotia and eastern Prince Edward Island. The Canadian West had isolated pockets of French Canadians as well. In fact, colonies had been established in the early 1800s on Hudson's Bay Company land on the prairie fringe, primarily to exploit the fur trade.

The itinerant Métis [who were part native American and part European] were a significant ethnic element of the fur trading population. Because they were French speaking and Roman Catholic, these fiercely independent descendants of the coureurs de bois identified with the French rather than the English peoples of Eastern Canada. For more than a century, they had been principals in the western fur trade, living in many cases an Indian way of life. As fur trading declined during the first half of the century, the Métis became progressively more dependent upon the buffalo for their livelihood. By the 1860s, however, the number of buffalo had declined significantly due to over exploitation and the impact of waves of settlers pouring into the Great Plains and prairies.

The policy—some would say obsession—of the new central

government in Ottawa was to occupy the Canadian West as quickly as possible to keep the region from being colonized by U.S. settlers, who had already begun to move northward across the border. Unfortunately, these settlers—European, U.S. and Canadian alike—came in direct contact and conflict with the Métis. At first diplomatically, and later violently, the Métis resisted attempts by the aggressive central government to destroy the buffalo and their habitat in order to build railways, subdivide the land and impose a sedentary way of life upon them.

In 1868, the government attempted to establish a new province out of the Red River settlement headquartered at Fort Gary (later Winnipeg), where the Métis were heavily concentrated. Under Louis Riel, their undisputed leader and one of the few free spirits and eccentrics in Canadian history, the Métis formed their own provisional government and insisted upon entering the Canadian union on their own terms. Several ugly incidents occurred before an agreement was negotiated that recognized Métis land claims and guaranteed French language rights and the free practice of the Roman Catholic Religion. This led to the passage of the Manitoba Act and the creation of Canada's fifth province.

Riel reappeared in Saskatchewan during the mid-1880s to defend and protect once again the Métis and Indian way of life in what was then the "western frontier." Riel was captured, convicted of treason and hanged. This action elicited a considerable backlash against the English, particularly in Quebec, since Riel's hanging was seen as an act of irrational vengeance against French Catholic people by the English Protestant establishment of Ontario.

Riel's demise marked the end of Indian, Métis and French power in the West and paved the way for the abrogation of their civil rights in Manitoba a few years later. The francophones were subsequently overwhelmed by the massive infusion of English colonists; by 1900, only isolated pockets were left, mainly in southern Manitoba near Winnipeg (St. Boniface).

By the turn of the century, the Province of Quebec was increasingly identified as the heartland of French Canada. The French population continued to produce at an enormous rate, equivalent to the indigenous growth of the English population plus immigration. While this distinctive province functioned comfortably within the Canadian Confederation, its societal development and politics periodically diverged from the central government.

Outmigration from the farms in Quebec to the cities, the West or the United States continued. The church-inspired frontier development policy north of the St. Lawrence had failed to attract enough settlers to have any significant impact upon this rural-to-urban rush. Foundries, breweries, textile factories and banks, controlled primarily by the English minority in the province, flourished in the towns and cities. Although a small industrial and financial French Canadian bourgeoisie existed in the urban areas, the majority of the population was still rural and tied closely to the church and *la terre* [the earth]. Quebec, therefore, entered the 20th century different in many respects from the English-speaking provinces. It lagged behind the rest of Canada, especially Ontario, in industrial development with a people still clinging to traditional values and life-style.

The Case for Québécois Sovereignty

By René Lévesque

In the 1960s, after a long period of relative isolation and insularity, Quebec underwent a transformation known as the Quiet Revolution. The shift from a rural existence centered on farming, family, and church toward a more urban, open society was unmistakable, and was accompanied by a flourishing in arts, culture, education, and politics. One of the key figures to emerge during this period was René Lévesque, who became a prominent politician and proponent of a separate, sovereign Quebec. In the following article, drawn from his 1968 book, the English title of which is An Option for Quebec, *Lévesque outlines his view of Quebec's history and his vision of its future. For Lévesque, only a sovereign Quebec could protect and preserve the French language and culture, which he and many others saw as increasingly threatened by the advent of mass communications on a continent where the French are a tiny minority. Lévesque argues that a new political association between a sovereign Canada and a sovereign Quebec, which he calls a Canadian Union, would best serve the interests of both the English and the French.*

We are *Québécois.*

What that means first and foremost—and if need be, all that it means—is that we are attached to this one corner of the earth where we can be completely ourselves: this Quebec, the only place where we have the unmistakable feeling that "here we can be really at home."

Being ourselves is essentially a matter of keeping and developing a personality that has survived for three and a half centuries.

At the core of this personality is the fact that we speak French.

Everything else depends on this one essential element and follows from it or leads us infallibly back to it.

In our history, America began with a French look, briefly but gloriously given it by Champlain, Joliet, La Salle, La-Verendrye [early French explorers]. . . . We learn our first lessons in progress and perseverance from Maisonneuve, Jeanne Mance, Jean Talon; and in daring or heroism from Lambert Closse, Brébeuf, Frontenac, d'Iberville [early French explorers, missionaries, and settlers].

Then came the conquest. We were a conquered people, our hearts set on surviving in some small way on a continent that had become Anglo-Saxon.

Somehow or other, through countless changes and a variety of regimes, despite difficulties without number (our lack of awareness and even our ignorance serving all too often as our best protection), we succeeded. . . .

Until recently in this difficult process of survival we enjoyed the protection of a certain degree of isolation. We lived a relatively sheltered life in a rural society in which a great measure of unanimity reigned, and in which poverty set its limits on change and aspiration alike.

We are children of that society, in which the *habitant*, our father or grandfather, was still the key citizen. We also are heirs to that fantastic adventure—that early America that was almost entirely French. We are, even more intimately, heirs to the group obstinacy which has kept alive that portion of French America we call *Québec*.

All these things lie at the core of this personality of ours. Anyone who does not feel it, at least occasionally, is not—is no longer—one of us.

But *we* know and feel that these are the things that make us what we are. They enable us to recognize each other wherever we may be. This is our own special wave-length on which, despite all interference, we can tune each other in loud and clear, with no one else listening. . . .

A Changing Society

On the other hand, one would have to be blind not to see that the conditions under which this personality must assert itself have changed in our lifetime, at an extremely rapid and still accelerating rate.

Our traditional society, which gave our parents the security of an environment so ingrown as to be reassuring and in which many of us grew up in a way that we thought could, with care, be preserved indefinitely; that "quaint old" society has gone.

Today, most of us are city dwellers, wage-earners, tenants. The standards of parish, village, and farm have been splintered. The automobile and the airplane take us "outside" in a way we never could have imagined thirty years ago, or even less. Radio and films, and now television, have opened for us a window onto everything that goes on throughout the world: the events—and the ideas too—of all humanity invade our homes day after day.

The age of automatic unanimity thus has come to an end. The old protective barriers are less and less able to mark safe pathways for our lives. The patience and resignation that were preached to us in the old days with such efficiency now produce no other reactions than scepticism or indifference, or even rebellion.

At our own level, we are going through a universal experience. In this sudden acceleration of history, whose main features are the unprecedented development of science, technology, and economic activity, there are potential promises and dangers immeasurably greater than any the world ever has known.

The promises—if man so desires—are those of abundance, of liberty, of fraternity; in short, of a civilization that could attain heights undreamed of by the most unrestrained Utopians.

The dangers—unless man can hold them in check—are those of insecurity and servitude, of inhuman governments, of conflicts among nations that could lead to extermination.

In this little corner of ours, we already are having a small taste of the dangers as well as the promises of this age.

The dangers are striking enough.

In a world where, in so many fields, the only stable law seems to have become that of perpetual change, where our old certainties are crumbling one after the other, we find ourselves swept along helplessly by irresistible currents. We are not at all sure that we can stay afloat, for the swift, confusing pace of events forces us to realize as never before our own weaknesses, our backwardness, our terrible collective vulnerability.

Endlessly, with a persistence almost masochistic, we draw up list after list of our inadequacies. For too long we despised education. We lack scientists, administrators, qualified technical people. Economically, we are colonials whose three meals a day depend far too much on the initiative and goodwill of foreign bosses. And we must admit as well that we are far from being the most advanced along the path of social progress, the yardstick by which the quality of a human community can best be measured. For a very long time we have allowed our public administration to stagnate in negligence and corruption, and left our political life in the hands of fast talkers and our own equivalent of those African kings who grew rich by selling their own tribesmen. . . .

A Vision for the Future

The only way to overcome the danger is to face up to this trying and thoughtless age and make it accept us as we are, succeeding somehow in making a proper and appropriate place in it for ourselves, in our own language, so that we can feel we are equals and not inferiors. This means that in our homeland we must be able to earn our living and pursue our careers in French. It also means that we must build a society which, while it preserves an image that is our own, will be as progressive, as efficient, and as "civilized" as any in the world. (In fact, there are other small peoples who are showing us the way, demonstrating that maximum size is in no way synonymous with maximum progress among human societies.)

To speak plainly, we must give ourselves sufficient reason to be not only sure of ourselves but also, perhaps, a little proud. Now, in the last few years we have indeed made some progress along this difficult road of "catching up," the road which leads to the greater promise of our age.

At least enough progress to know that what comes next depends only on ourselves and on the choices that only we can make.

The enticements toward progress were phrases like "from now on," or "it's got to change," or "masters in our own house," etc.

The results can be seen on every side. Education, for us as for any people desirous of maintaining its place in the world, has finally become the top priority. With hospital insurance, family and school allowances, pension schemes, and the beginnings of medicare, our social welfare has made more progress in a few years than in the whole preceding century; and for the first time we find ourselves, in many of the most important areas, ahead of the rest of the country. In the economic field, by nationalizing electric power, by creating the S.G.F. [la Société Générale de Financement, a company designed to promote business in Quebec],

Soquem, [a government-owned mining company] and the *Caisse de Dépôts* [the investment arm of the Quebec Pension Plan] we have taken the first steps toward the kind of collective control of certain essential services without which no human community can feel secure. We also, at last, have begun to clean up our electoral practices, to modernize and strengthen our administrative structures, to give our land the roads that are indispensable to its future, and to study seriously the complex problems of our outmoded municipalities and underdeveloped regions. . . .

But in the process we have learned certain things, things which are both simple and revolutionary.

The first is that we have the capacity to do the job ourselves, and the more we take charge and accept our responsibilities, the more efficient we find we are; capable, all things considered, of succeeding just as well as anyone else.

Another is that there is no valid *excuse*, that it is up to us to find and apply to our problems the solutions that are right for us; for no one else can, much less wants to, solve them for us.

Yet another thing we have learned—and perhaps the most important: "The appetite comes with the eating." This is a phenomenon we can see everywhere as soon as a human group decides to move forward. It is called the "revolution of rising expectations."

This is the main driving force at our disposal for continued progress. We must calculate its use as precisely as possible, to avoid costly diversions; but even more we must take care not to stifle it, for without this we shall experience the collective catastrophe of an immobilized society, at a time when those who fail to advance automatically retreat, and to a point which can easily become one of no return.

In other words, above all we must guard against loss of impetus, against the periodic desire to slow down, against the belief that we are moving too quickly when in reality—despite a few wanderings—we are just beginning to reach the speed our age demands. In this, a nation is like an individual: those who succeed are those who are unafraid of life. . . .

Two Nations, One Country

We are a nation within a country where there are two nations. For all the things we mentioned earlier, using words like "individuality," "history," "society," and "people," are also the things one includes under the word "nation." It means nothing more

LORD DURHAM'S CALL FOR FRENCH ASSIMILATION

After rebellions broke out in Canada in 1837, the British Parliament appointed Lord Durham to investigate and report on the conditions in the colonies. The Durham Report of 1839 is widely recognized as one of the most important documents in Canadian history, in part because Durham recommends that the Canadian colonies move toward a system of independent government. As the following excerpt shows, however, French Canadians remember the report for a different reason.

I expected to find a contest between a government and a people: I found two nations warring in the bosom of a single state: I found a struggle, not of principles, but of races; and I perceived that it would be idle to attempt any amelioration of laws or institutions until we could first succeed in terminating the deadly animosity that now separates the inhabitants of Lower Canada into the hostile divisions of French and English. . . .

I entertain no doubts as to the national character which must be given to Lower Canada; it must be that of the British Empire; that of the majority of the population of British America; that of the great race which must in the lapse of no long period of time be predominant over the whole North American Continent. Without effecting the change so rapidly or so roughly as to shock the feelings and trample on the welfare of the existing generation, it must henceforth be the first and steady purpose of the British Government to establish an English population, with English laws and language, in this Province, and to trust its government to none but a decidedly English Legislature. . . .

At the best, the fate of the educated and aspiring colonist is, at present, one of little hope, and little activity; but the French Canadian is cast still further into the shade, by a language and habits foreign to those of the Imperial Government. . . . I desire the amalgamation still more for the sake of the humbler classes. Their present state of rude and equal plenty is fast deteriorating under the pressure of population in the narrow limits to which they are confined. If they attempt to better their condition, by extending themselves over the neighbouring country, they will necessarily get more and more mingled with an English population: if they prefer remaining stationary, the greater part of them must be labourers in the employ of English capitalists. In either case it would appear that the great mass of the French Canadians are doomed, in some measure, to occupy an inferior position, and to be dependent on the English for employment. The evils of poverty and dependence would merely be aggravated in a ten-fold degree, by a spirit of jealous and resentful nationality, which should separate the working class of the community from the possessors of wealth and employers of labour. . . .

There can hardly be conceived a nationality more destitute of all that can invigorate and elevate a people, than that which is exhibited by the descendants of the French in Lower Canada, owing to their retaining their peculiar language and manners. They are a people with no history, and no literature. The literature of England is written in a language which is not theirs; and the only literature which their language renders familiar to them, is that of a nation from which they have been separated by eighty years of a foreign rule and still more by those changes which the Revolution and its consequences have wrought in the whole political, moral, and social state of France. . . .

In these circumstances, I should be indeed surprised if the more reflecting part of the French Canadians entertained at present any hope of continuing to preserve their nationality.

Report on the Affairs of British North America from the Earl of Durham . . . Presented by Her Majesty's Command, reprinted in Donald C. Masters, *A Short History of Canada.* Princeton, NJ: Van Nostrand, 1958.

than the collective will to live that belongs to any national entity likely to survive.

Two nations in a single country: this means, as well, that in fact there are *two majorities*, two "complete societies" quite distinct from each other trying to get along within a common framework. That this number puts us in a minority position makes no difference: just as a civilized society will never condemn a little man to feel inferior beside a bigger man, civilized relations among nations demand that they treat each other as equals in law and in fact.

Now we believe it to be evident that the hundred-year-old framework of Canada can hardly have any effect other than to create increasing difficulties between the two parties insofar as their mutual respect and understanding are concerned, as well as impeding the changes and progress so essential to both.

It is useless to go back over the balance sheet of the century just past, listing the advantages it undoubtedly has brought us and the obstacles and injustices it even more unquestionably has set in our way.

The important thing for today and for tomorrow is that both sides realize that this regime has had its day, and that it is a matter of urgency either to modify it profoundly or to build a new one. . . .

For the present regime also prevents the English-speaking majority from simplifying, rationalizing, and centralizing as it would like to do certain institutions which it, too, realizes are obsolete. This is an ordeal which English Canada is finding more and more exhausting, and for which it blames to the exaggerated anxieties and the incorrigible intransigence of Quebec.

It is clear, we believe, that this frustration may easily become intolerable. And it is precisely among the most progressive and "nationalist" groups in English Canada, among those who are concerned about the economic, cultural, and political invasion from the United States, among those who are seeking the means to prevent the country from surrendering completely, that there is the greatest risk of a growing and explosive resentment toward Quebec for the reasons mentioned above.

A New Quebec

And these are the very men among whom we should be able to find the best partners for our dialogue over the new order that must emerge.

We are seeking at last to carve out for ourselves a worthy and acceptable place in this Quebec which has never belonged to us as it should have. Facing us, however, a growing number of our fellow-citizens of the other majority are afraid of losing the homeland that Canada was for them in the good old days of the Empire, when they at least had the impression that they were helping to rule, and that it was all within the family. Today the centres of decision-making are shifting south of the border at a terrifying rate.

In this parallel search for two national securities, as long as the search is pursued within the present system or anything remotely resembling it, we can end up only with double paralysis. The two majorities, basically desiring the same thing—a chance to live their own lives, in their own way, according to their own needs and aspirations—will inevitably collide with one another repeatedly and with greater and greater force, causing hurts that finally would be irreparable.

As long as we persist so desperately in maintaining—with spit and chewing gum or whatever—the ancient hobble of a federalism suited to the last century, the two nations will go on creating an ever-growing jungle of compromises while disagreeing more and more strongly on essentials.

This would mean a perpetual atmosphere of instability, of wrangling over everything and over nothing. It would mean the sterilization of two collective "personalities" which, having squandered the most precious part of their potential, would weaken each other so completely that they would have no other choice but to drown themselves in the ample bosom of "America."

We think it is possible for both parties to avoid this blind alley. We must have the calm courage to see that the problem can't be solved either by maintaining or somehow adapting the *status quo*. One is always somewhat scared at the thought of leaving a home in which one has lived for a long time. It becomes almost "consecrated," and all the more so in this case, because what we call "Confederation" is one of the last remnants of those age-old safeguards of which modern times have robbed us. It is therefore quite normal that some people cling to it with a kind of desperation that arises far more from fear than from reasoned attachment.

But there are moments—and this is one of them—when courage and calm daring become the only proper form of prudence that a people can exercise in a crucial period of its existence. If it fails at these times to accept the calculated risk of the great leap, it may miss its vocation forever, just as does a man who is afraid of life.

What should we conclude from a cool look at the crucial crossroads that we now have reached? Clearly that we must rid ourselves completely of a completely obsolete federal regime.

And begin anew.

Begin how?

The answer, it seems to us, is as clearly written as the question, in the two great trends of our age: that of the freedom of peoples, and that of the formation by common consent of economic and political groupings.

A Sovereign Quebec

For our own good, we must dare to seize for ourselves complete liberty in Quebec, the right to all the essential components of independence, *i.e.,* the complete mastery of every last area of basic collective decision-making.

This means that Quebec must become sovereign as soon as possible.

Thus we finally would have within our grasp the security of our collective "being" which is so vital to us, a security which otherwise must remain uncertain and incomplete.

Then it will be up to us, and us alone, to establish calmly, without recrimination or discrimination, the priority for which we are now struggling feverishly but blindly: that of our language and our culture.

Only then will we have the opportunity—and the obligation—to use our talents to the maximum in order to resolve without further excuses or evasions all the great problems that confront us, whether it be a negotiated protective system for our farmers, or decent treatment for our employees and workers in industry, or the form and evolution of the political structures we must create for ourselves.

In short, this is not for us simply the only solution to the present Canadian impasse; it also is the one and only common goal inspiring enough to bring us together with the kind of strength and unity we shall need to confront all possible futures—the supreme challenge of continuous progress within a society that has taken control of its own destiny.

As for the other Canadian majority, it will also find our solution to its advantage, for it will be set free at once from the constraints imposed on it by our presence; it will be at liberty in its own way to rebuild to its heart's desire the political institutions of English Canada and to prove to itself, whether or not it really wants to maintain and develop on this continent, an English-speaking society distinct from the United States.

A New Canadian Union

And if this is the case, there is no reason why we, as future neighbours, should not voluntarily remain associates and partners in a common enterprise; which would conform to the second great trend of our times: the new economic groups, customs unions, common markets, etc.

Here we are talking about something which already exists, for it is composed of the bonds, the complementary activities, the many forms of economic co-operation within which we have learned to live. Nothing says that we must throw these things away; on the contrary, there is every reason to maintain the framework. If we destroyed it, interdependent as we are, we would only be obliged sooner or later to build it up again, and then with doubtful success. . . .

We are not sailing off into uncharted seas. Leaving out the gigantic model furnished by the evolution of the Common Market, we can take our inspiration from countries comparable in size to our own—Benelux or Scandinavia—among whom cooperation is highly advanced, and where it has promoted unprecedented progress in the member states without preventing any of them from continuing to live according to their own tradition and preferences.

To sum up, we propose a system that would allow our two majorities to extricate themselves from an archaic federal framework in which our two very distinct "personalities" paralyze each other by dint of pretending to have a third personality common to both.

This new relationship of two nations, one with its homeland in Quebec and another free to rearrange the rest of the country at will, would be freely associated in a new adaptation of the current "common-market" formula, making up an entity which could perhaps—and if so very precisely—be called a Canadian Union.

The future of a people is never born without effort. It requires that a rather large number of "midwives" knowingly make the grave decision to work at it. For apart from other blind forces, and apart from all the imponderables, we must believe that basically it is still men who make man's history.

What we are suggesting to those who want to listen is that we devote our efforts, together, to shape the history of Quebec in the only fitting direction; and we are certain that at the same time we shall also be helping the rest of the country to find a better future of its own.

Canada's New Constitution and the Quebec Separatist Movement

By Peter H. Russell

Although the Canadian confederation dates to 1867, it was not until 1982 that the constitution was patriated, which gave Canadians, rather than the British Parliament, control over its amendment. In this article, Peter H. Russell, professor emeritus of political science at the University of Toronto, reflects on the meaning of patriation and on the twenty years that followed it. According to Russell, many Quebecers deeply resented the fact that the new constitution did not grant their province a veto over future constitutional change. The decade immediately following patriation witnessed several attempts to placate Quebecers and others dissatisfied with patriation. Although these attempts for the most part failed, and there are some lingering constitutional issues, Russell argues that the nation as a whole has flourished.

On April 17 [1982], twenty years ago, beneath a brooding grey Ottawa sky, Queen Elizabeth II signed the Canada Act patriating Canada's Constitution. The ominous weather matched the political mood of the day. The efforts of [Prime Minister] Pierre Trudeau and his colleagues to make this day on which Canada completed its evolution to constitutional independence one of national celebration could not dissipate the political clouds. The title of a major collection of

Peter H. Russell, "Patriation: We Have Succeeded Despite Ourselves," *The Beaver: Exploring Canada's History*, vol. 82, April/May 2002, p. 6. Copyright © 2002 by Peter H. Russell. Reproduced by permission.

essays by Canadian scholars analyzing the significance of the event said it all—*And No One Cheered*. The Constitution had come home, but to a home still bitterly divided on constitutional fundamentals.

Patriation itself seemed on the surface to be such a simple and obvious exercise. Constitutional patriation meant that Canada's Constitution would no longer have the status of an imperial act amendable by the imperial Parliament in Westminster but would be a set of Canadian laws amendable entirely in Canada. That this change did not take place until late in the twentieth century had nothing to do with Britain's wanting to hold on to the strings of imperial power. After all, at the beginning of the twentieth century, when the Australian federation was established, Britain was happy to leave Australia's new constitution in the hands of the Australian people. No, Canada's delay in taking custody of its Constitution was not due to British recalcitrance but to our own inability to agree on the kind of a people we are.

This point requires a little explanation. In a constitutional democracy—which in spirit Canada had become long before patriation in 1982—the written Constitution is the country's highest law. Whoever, or whatever, can make changes in that highest law is the country's highest— i.c., sovereign—political authority. Among a democratic people, constitutional sovereignty must be held by the people themselves or by those directly accountable to the people. Patriation of Canada's Constitution meant replacing the imperial Parliament as our constitutional sovereign with a democratic Canadian sovereign. But who or what in Canada can act for the Canadian people? Where is sovereignty in Canada to be located? It was the failure of Canadians to agree on an answer to that question that postponed patriation for so long.

Dividing Power

For many Canadians, answering this question may seem easy— vest constitutional sovereignty in a majority of Canadians or the Canadian Parliament elected by a majority of Canadians. But there are many other Canadians with articulate and powerful leaders, like provincial premiers, who would never accept this answer. They would—and did—insist that Canada is a federal country in which the people are also represented through provincial legislatures, and therefore the provinces must have a share of constitutional sovereignty. If it were proposed—as indeed it was—

that constitutional sovereignty be shared by the federal parliament and provincial legislatures representing a majority of Canadians, Quebec leaders elected to govern that province would insist— and did—that since their province is the homeland of one of Canada's founding peoples, a simple majority of provinces was not enough—Quebec itself must have a veto over any constitutional changes affecting its powers. By the 1970s, Canada's aboriginal peoples were also demanding recognition and a role in any constitutional changes concerning them.

This profound question of deciding on the locus of constitutional sovereignty in our country was referred to by political leaders and journalists in classically untheoretical, understated Canadianese as the problem of finding an amending formula—as if it were like finding a good recipe for a cake. The amending formula question became ever so much more difficult to resolve consensually when political leaders, first in Quebec, then in Ottawa, and after that virtually everywhere else, became convinced that patriation should be accompanied by a wholesale restructuring of the Constitution to fulfill their "vision" of Canada. The trouble, of course, was that these leaders, like the people they represent, harboured very different visions of constitutional perfection. Through the 1970s much political energy was spent on trying to reach a broad consensus on patriation and constitutional reform. Finally, in October 1980, Pierre Trudeau, fresh from his victory over the Quebec separatists and tired of negotiating with the provincial premiers, announced that his government—with or without the provinces—would proceed to patriate the Canadian Constitution on the basis of his "people's package" of constitutional reforms.

The people's package contained three principal components. First—and foremost in Trudeau's appeal to the people—was the Canadian Charter of Rights and Freedoms. Second was recognition of the rights of Canada's aboriginal peoples. Third was a formula for amending Canada's Constitution entirely in Canada—the key to patriation. Though many Canadians had the impression that Canada was adopting a new Constitution in 1982, these three elements, plus a tiny increment of power to the provinces over trade in natural resources, were the only substantial changes patriation effected in Canada's Constitution. The old original BNA [British North America] Act—now repackaged as the Constitution Act 1867—was still intact.

Quebec Says No

Trudeau was prodded first by the British Parliament (which had to agree to sever the umbilical cord) and then by the Supreme Court of Canada to seek the provinces' approval of his people's package. By making a few changes, he was able to secure the support of all the provinces except Quebec. Not only did the people's package make no concessions to Quebec's demands for special status, it denied Quebec a veto over constitutional changes affecting its powers. On November 25, 1981, the Quebec National Assembly [as the Quebec provincial assembly is called], with support from federalists as well as sovereignists, passed a decree rejecting the patriation package. While the decree had no legal force, it was the darkest cloud on Canada's political horizon.

Patriation was followed by a frantic decade of constitutional politics as Canada's political leaders endeavoured to secure constitutional changes designed to meet the discontents left over from patriation. First came a 1983 conference with aboriginal leaders that produced agreement on a constitutional amendment recognizing land-claim agreements as constitutionally protected treaties. This was the first time the new patriated amending system was put to use. From there on in it was all downhill. The three aboriginal-focused conferences that followed failed to reach agreement on recognizing the aboriginal peoples' inherent right to govern their own societies. Then in 1987 came the struggle to "bring Quebec back into the constitutional family" by adopting the Meech Lake Accord that, among other things, would recognize Quebec as a "distinct society" and restore Quebec's constitutional veto. When the three-year time limit for ratification ran out in 1990 with Manitoba and Newfoundland still not agreeing, we moved on to an heroic attempt to please everyone with a huge bundle of constitutional changes—the Charlottetown Accord. This effort culminated in rejection of the Charlottetown Accord in the October 1992 referendum.

A Quiet Decade

In our first decade of patriation, Canadians learned—the hard way—that being free from imperial encumbrances in our constitutional affairs does not free us from our internal divisions. Just as importantly, we learned how destructively distracting it can be to try to heal these differences by seeking agreement on a big constitutional deal—all the more so when there is an insistence on popular ratification of important constitutional changes. And so the second decade of patriation, except for the 1995 Quebec referendum, has been relatively quiescent constitutionally speaking. The rancour and indecisiveness of the 1995 referendum may even have cured Quebecers of the constitutional fever.

Abandoning the quest for a big-bang resolution of constitutional differences has not put Canada into a constitutional deep freeze. The new patriated amending process has been used to make changes of regional importance—such as recognizing New Brunswick's bicultural nature, removing Newfoundland and Quebec from the shackles of obsolete denominational education guarantees, and enabling Prince Edward Island to trade in a steamboat for a bridge link to mainland Canada. We have used more informal instruments of constitutional change to enable the Inuit of the Eastern Arctic to enjoy home rule in Nunavut, to facilitate our adjustment to globalization by removing internal and external barriers to free trade, and to put federal-provincial relations on a more cooperative footing in a new social union. Quebec's opting out of the latter without fiscal penalty provides de facto recognition of the special status it could not win de jure.

Two decades after taking charge of our own constitutional affairs, we Canadians have learned an important lesson about the Constitution. It is possible for our country not only to survive but to be a relatively prosperous and peaceful homeland for us all and a constructive member of the international community, even though we may well remain divided on some constitutional fundamentals. In this sense, patriation has succeeded despite ourselves.

Chrétien's Call for a United Canada

By Jean Chrétien

Although a solid majority of voters in the first Quebec referendum on sovereignty, in 1980, rejected separation, by the 1990s there were renewed calls for a sovereign Quebec and the issue again came to a provincial referendum. On the evening of October 25, 1995, just days before the October 30 referendum, Prime Minister Jean Chrétien, Québécois by birth, addressed the country on national television. In his speech, which is reprinted below, Chrétien appeals to Quebec voters to choose to remain Canadians. He argues that although the country is not perfect, its success at providing its citizens with peace and security is unmatched by any other country in the world. Furthermore, Chrétien insists that although French Canadians deserve to have their language and culture protected, a united Canada, with Quebec as one part, will best be able to do that. In his speech, Chrétien also asks Canadians living outside of Quebec to express to Quebecers how important their presence is to the rest of Canada. In the October 30 referendum, Quebec voted not to separate by a margin of 1 percent.

For the first time in my mandate as Prime Minister, I have asked to speak directly to Canadians tonight [October 25, 1995].

I do so because we are in an exceptional situation.

Tonight, in particular, I want to speak to my fellow Quebecers. Because, at this moment, the future of our whole country is in their hands.

But I also want to speak to all Canadians. Because this issue concerns them—deeply. It is not only the future of Quebec that will be decided on Monday. It is the future of all of Canada. The decision that will be made is serious and irreversible. With deep, deep consequences.

Jean Chrétien, "Address to the Nation," http://collections.ic.gc.ca, October 25, 1995.

What is at stake is our country. What is at stake is our heritage. To break up Canada or build Canada. To remain Canadian or no longer be Canadian. To stay or to leave. This is the issue of the referendum.

When my fellow Quebecers make their choice on Monday, they have the responsibility and the duty to understand the implications of that choice.

The fact is, that hidden behind a murky question is a very clear option. It is the separation of Quebec. A Quebec that would no longer be part of Canada. Where Quebecers would no longer enjoy the rights and privileges associated with Canadian citizenship. Where Quebecers would no longer share a Canadian passport or a Canadian dollar—no matter what the advocates of separatism may claim.

Where Quebecers would be made foreigners in their own country.

I know that many Quebecers, in all good faith, are thinking of voting YES in order to bring change to Canada. I am telling them that if they wish to remain Canadian, they are taking a very dangerous gamble. Anyone who really wants to remain a Canadian should think twice before taking such a dangerous risk. Listen to the leaders of the separatist side. They are very clear. The country they want is not a better Canada, it is a separate Quebec. Don't be fooled.

There are also those Quebecers who are thinking of voting YES to give Quebec a better bargaining position to negotiate an economic and political partnership with the rest of Canada. Again, don't be fooled. A YES vote means the destruction of the political and economic union we already enjoy. Nothing more.

Through the course of this campaign, I have listened to my fellow Quebecers, and I have heard them say how deeply attached they are to Canada. I have listened—and I understand—that they have been hurt and disappointed in the past. I have also heard the voices for change that are echoing throughout Quebec and across Canada. Our country is changing. And we all know it. I ask you to remember all that this government has done over the last two years to help create change—positive change.

The End of a Dream

The end of Canada would be nothing less than the end of a dream. The end of a country that has made us the envy of the world. Canada is not just any country. It is unique. It is the best country in the world.

Perhaps it is something we have come to take for granted. But we should never, never let that happen. Once more, today it's up to each of us to restate our love for Canada. To say we don't want to lose it.

What we have built together in Canada is something very great and very noble. A country whose values of tolerance, understanding, generosity have made us what we are: a society where our number one priority is the respect and dignity of all our citizens.

Other countries invest in weapons, we invest in the well-being of our citizens. Other countries tolerate poverty and despair, we work hard to ensure a basic level of decency for everyone. Other countries resort to violence to settle differences, we work out our problems through compromise and mutual respect.

This is what we have accomplished.

And I say to my fellow Quebecers don't let anyone diminish or take away what we have accomplished. Don't let anyone tell you that you cannot be a proud Quebecer and a proud Canadian.

It is true Canada is not perfect. But I cannot think of a single place in the world that comes closer. Not a single place where people lead better lives. Where they live in greater peace and security.

Why does Canada work? Because our country has always been able to adapt and change to meet the hopes and aspirations of our citizens. We've done so in the past. We're doing so today. And we will continue to do so in the future.

A Distinct Society

And I repeat tonight what I said yesterday in Verdun. We must recognize that Quebec's language, its culture and institutions make it a distinct society. And no constitutional change that affects the powers of Quebec should ever be made without the consent of Quebecers.

And that all governments—federal and provincial—must respond to the desire of Canadians—everywhere—for greater decentralization.

And all that can happen quietly, calmly, without rupture—with determination.

To all Canadians outside Quebec, I say do not lose faith in this country. And continue to show the respect, the openness, the attachment, and the friendship you have shown to your fellow Canadians in Quebec all through the referendum campaign.

Continue to tell them how important they are to you. And how without them, Canada would no longer be Canada. How you want them to remain Canadian and you hope, deeply and profoundly, that they choose Canada on Monday.

In recent days, thousands of Canadians have taken the time to send messages of friendship and attachment to Quebecers. Keep them coming.

My friends, once again, our country is facing a crisis. And crisis and uncertainty exact a very heavy cost. We all pay a high price for political instability.

On Monday, once Quebecers have shown their commitment to Canada, I want to ask Canadian investors and foreign investors to show their commitment and confidence in return.

Together, we will need to get our priorities back on track. On economic growth and jobs. And the time is long overdue.

My friends, we are facing a decisive moment in the history of our country.

And people all across Canada know that decision lies in the hands of their fellow Canadians in Quebec.

A United Canada

As a proud Quebecer and a proud Canadian, I am convinced that a strong Quebec in a united Canada remains the best solution for all of us. I ask those Quebecers who have not yet made their decision to ask themselves these questions when they vote on Monday:

Do you really think that you and your family would have a better quality of life and a brighter future in a separate Quebec?

Do you really think that the French language and culture in North America would be better protected in a separate Quebec?

Do you really think you and your family will enjoy greater security in a separate Quebec?

Do you really want to turn your back on Canada? Does Canada deserve that?

Are you really ready to tell the world—the whole world—that people of different languages, different cultures and different backgrounds cannot live together in harmony?

Do you really think that ties of friendship and understanding

. . . ties of mutual trust and respect can be broken without harm or rancour?

Have you found one reason, one good reason, to destroy Canada?

Do you really think it is worth abandoning the country we have built, and which our ancestors have left us?

Do you really think it makes any sense—any sense at all—to break up Canada?

These are the questions I ask each of you to consider. It's a big, very big responsibility.

In a few days, all the shouting will be over. And at that moment, you will be alone to make your decision. At that moment I urge you, my fellow Quebecers, to listen to your heart—and to your head.

I am confident that Quebec and Canada will emerge strong and united.

Thank you. And good night.

Quebec Nationalism and the 1995 Referendum

BY SCOTT KEMP

When the separatists lost the 1995 referendum in Quebec, the provincial premier Jacques Parizeau blamed the loss on "money and the ethnic vote." In the following article, Scott Kemp, who as a newspaper reporter covered the Quebec Referendum in 1995, analyzes the referendum and argues that Parizeau was right. Large businesses, which is what Parizeau meant by "money," are naturally wary of political instability, Kemp contends. Furthermore, according to Kemp, the "ethnic vote"—Quebec residents who are not descendants of the first French settlers—saw little reason to favor a nationalism based on French ethnicity. At the heart of the problem concerning Quebec, Kemp believes, are two competing visions of nationalism. The one that prevails in English Canada, he argues, is civic nationalism, in which a nation is defined by a constitutional structure and a code of laws. As Kemp sees it, however, nationalism based on ethnicity prevails among those in favor of sovereignty for Quebec. The question facing Canada, he believes, is whether it can accommodate these two competing views of nationalism.

M oney and the ethnic vote. No comment was more vilified than Jacques Parizeau's snap assessment of his side's razor-thin defeat in the 1995 Quebec referendum.

But reaction has been virtually all criticism—and no analysis. The reason is simple: Any analysis would inevitably conclude that Parizeau's comments were right on the money. And the ethnic vote.

Scott Kemp, "L'argent et la vote ethnique," *Canada: Our Country, Our Lives*, Spring 1997. Copyright © 1997 by *The Queen's Journal*. Reproduced by permission.

Business, especially big business, doesn't like political instability, and secession is about as unstable as you can get. Therefore,
business, or "money," if you will, tends to be leery of Quebec
separatism. No surprises there.

The issue that dares not speak its name, though, is the so-called
ethnic vote: the fact non-francophone Quebeckers, be they English, Jewish, Italian, or Lebanese, see no advantage to supporting
a separate Quebec. The reason for this is simple, too—Quebec
separatism is a matter of ethnic nationalism. The descendants of
the French settlers along the St. Lawrence River see themselves
as a nation, as an identifiable group with its own language, culture, and history, like the Jews, the Scots, or the Japanese. Like
most other "nationalists" in the world, many Québecois want
their own country devoted to preserving linguistic and cultural
distinctiveness.

Ethnic Nationalism

This is, of course, where English Canadians, "ethnics," and other
opponents of separatism get squeamish. Is it right to create a state
for the sake of one dominant ethnic group? Among English
Canadians and federalist Quebeckers, the answer is a resounding
no. Some opponents of separatism, notably former Prime Minister Pierre Trudeau, even equate separatism with racism.

This, however, is unfair. Separatism may certainly be bad for
Canada, unpatriotic, unconstitutional, and even traitorous, but it
is not racist.

To condemn all nation states is to condemn many of the
world's most tolerant countries. After all, what is Sweden if not a
state for Swedes? Norway even went so far as to separate from
Sweden early this century, hence giving Norwegians a nation state
of their own. Yet these Scandinavian countries are generally recognized as two of the most progressive and tolerant in the world.

Of course, the twentieth century has seen the terrible consequences of extreme nationalism with Nazi Germany. However,
the culprit was extremism, not nationalism. If Sweden can be a
nation state without Nazism, so can Germany. And today it is.

Ethnic nationalism is also not unknown in English Canada.
Until the Second World War, English Canada was something of
an Anglo-Saxon nation state of its own. Such sentiment is deeply
rooted in our history.

Lord Durham, in his famous analysis of the 1837 rebellions,

described British North America as "two nations warring in the bosom of a single state." In 1867, Confederation was understood to rest upon "two founding nations." Subsequently, politicians like Sir John A. Macdonald often referred to Canada's "two founding races." (In Victorian parlance, "race" tended to denote ethnic, as opposed to physical, differences.)

And English Canada did behave much like a nation. Its citizens were largely of British origin and tended to view themselves as part of a larger Anglo-Saxon diaspora. They flew the Union Jack, sang "God Save the King," and enlisted to defend the Empire in both the Boer War and the Great War. In the early 1900s, plans even surfaced for a sort of "Imperial Federation" of Britain and Ireland, Canada, Australia, New Zealand, and South Africa. These so-called Anglo-Saxon countries were to share a foreign

---

QUEBEC SOVEREIGNTY REFERENDUMS

First in 1980, and then in 1995, the citizens of Quebec voted in a referendum on sovereignty. Both times, a majority voted to remain in Canada. As the following chart shows, however, in the most recent referendum there was greater voter turnout and the margin of victory was much slimmer.

	Percentage	Total Ballots
May 20, 1980		
For:	40.44%	1,485,851
Against:	59.56%	2,187,991
Majority:	19.11%	702,140
Participation Rate:	85.6%	3,738,854
October 30, 1995		
For:	49.42%	2,308,360
Against:	50.58%	2,362,648
Majority:	1.16%	54,288
Participation Rate:	93.52%	4,757,509

Chief Returning Officer, Quebec.

policy, military, and currency, all under the control of an "Imperial Parliament" in London. Of course, the Irish, the Dutch Afrikaaners, and the Québecois were not impressed.

Civic Nationalism

After the Second World War, this old, Imperial, English Canada began to unravel. A large wave of European immigration flooded Ontario, which had long been the bastion of Canadian "Anglo-Saxon-dom." Britain lost its Empire and began a long period of relative decline. Globalization replaced old Imperial trade routes. The United States, not Britain, became the dominant Western power of the Cold War. But perhaps most importantly, English Canadians changed, too. They shed a lingering colonial mentality to become an important "middle power" on the world stage.

This transformed English Canadian sentiments from the old Anglo-Saxon ethnic nationalism to what we now call "civic nationalism." English Canadians began to define their country in terms of federalism, constitutionalism, human rights and freedoms, diversity, and even social programs. Citizenship, not kinship, was the new guiding principle.

Unfortunately, Quebec's post-war transformation pushed it in almost the opposite direction. French Canadians stopped looking to the Catholic Church for social guidance and began to view their language and culture as their defining characteristics. Resentment over Canada's Imperial past and anglophone economic dominance further fuelled this re-invigorated nationalism. The Quiet Revolution had changed Québecois nationalism from strict devotion to strident emotion.

None of these changes, in Quebec or in the rest of Canada, was necessarily bad. In fact, they were invigorating and liberating. The only problem was that Quebec and English Canada became invigorated in opposite, almost irreconcilable ways. The result is a deeply divided country. English Canada is suspicious of a Quebec that won't become a fully integrated part of the Canadian civil state. Quebec is suspicious of a largely anglophone country that frowns upon French nationalism.

Is there a solution? Our ancestors designed a single state to accommodate two nations. Can we now design a state to accommodate two opposing views of nationalism itself? Or would a house so divided be truly unable to stand?

That is the question.

THE HISTORY OF NATIONS
Chapter 4

The Dream of
the Just Society

The Rise of the Welfare State

By J.M. Bumsted

In the following piece, J.M. Bumsted, a professor of history at the University of Manitoba, focuses on the rise of what is commonly known as the Canadian welfare state. The Second World War was followed by a period of growth and prosperity in Canada. According to Bumsted, the accompanying huge increase in the size of federal and provincial governments—which brought with it a wide range of social programs such as universal medical care, old-age pensions, and expanded educational opportunities—was not motivated by a clear vision of a welfare state promoting the good of its citizens. Bumsted maintains that the social safety net grew in fits and starts, as federal and provincial governments competed with one another and politicians sought to present the electorate with appealing platforms. Only under Prime Minister Pierre Trudeau, Bumsted argues, did the vision of the "Just Society" first become prominent. After Trudeau's election in 1968, the emphasis on social programs moved beyond ensuring a minimum standard of living to include greater income redistribution, and governments began to regularly spend more money than they received in taxes.

The post–Second World War era, particularly before 1960, was a period of unparalleled economic growth and prosperity for Canada. Production and consumption moved steadily upward. Employment rose almost continuously. Canada substantially increased its workforce. Inflation was steady but almost never excessive. Interest rates were relatively low. The nation was in the midst of an uncharacteristic natural increase in its population growth rate that would become known as the baby boom. At the same time that many Canadians took advantage of the good times by conceiving children and moving to new homes in the suburbs, both the federal and provincial governments became

J.M. Bumsted, *A History of the Canadian Peoples*. Toronto: Oxford University Press, 1998. Copyright © 1998 by Oxford University Press. Reproduced by permission.

active in providing new programs of social protection for their citizens. That network was not created without controversy, particularly of the constitutional variety, although the debate was still relatively muted until the 1960s. By that time, Canadian governments at all levels had become interventionist in a variety of ways, however, including the public nurture of culture. . . .

Government Grows

Government at all levels—federal, provincial, and municipal—grew extremely rapidly after the war. For the Dominion [of Canada] government, the extension of its power and authority represented a continuation of wartime momentum. For provincial governments, extensions of power were necessary to counter federal incursions in areas traditionally reserved for the provinces. All levels of government found the Canadian public responsive to the piecemeal introduction of new social services. The emergence of a much more powerful and costly public sector was fuelled partly by increased social programs, partly by the growth of a Canadian public-enterprise system after the war.

While the Canadian public-enterprise system went back to the nineteenth century, the development of Crown corporations [which are government run] greatly accelerated during and especially after the Second World War. Both federal and provincial governments created Crown corporations, publicly owned and operated. They modelled management structures on private enterprise and usually administered the corporation on a hands-off basis. Many Crown corporations came into existence to provide important services that could not be profitably offered by private enterprise. There was a tendency for public enterprise, almost by definition, to risk unprofitability. The CCF [Co-operative Commonwealth Federation, a socialist party] Saskatchewan government employed the Crown corporation frequently from the time of its election in 1944. One of the largest public enterprises of the 1950s, the St Lawrence Seaway, was a Crown corporation. For many rural Canadians the extension of electricity into all but the most remote corners of the country was a great development of the postwar period. Many provinces consolidated electric utilities in Crown corporations after the war to extend services. The federal government had hoped to expand Canada's social services after the Second World War, at least partly to justify continued control of the major tax fields it had acquired under wartime emergency conditions. At the Dominion-Provincial Conference on Reconstruction, which began on 6 August 1945 (the day the first atomic bomb was dropped on Japan), Ottawa discovered that not all the provinces were willing to withdraw permanently from the fields of personal and corporate income tax. Quebec and Ontario, particularly, were equally unenthusiastic about surrendering their constitutional rights to social services. The provincial rebuff to Ottawa in 1945 did not mean that the Dominion gave up on social security measures. Both funding and constitutional haggling, however, would be a continuing problem.

The Social Safety Net

While we often talk about the Canadian welfare state, there is little evidence that many people in Canada, much less in the federal government, had any notion of a truly comprehensive and integrated national social security system that would include full employment, housing, and education as part of the social rights of all Canadians. Social protection in Canada would instead grow on a piecemeal basis through the activities of all levels of government. Sometimes new programs responded to overt public demand, sometimes they met obvious public need. Frequently job creation was the immediate rationale for a social program. Ofttimes a particular program of social protection was intended to provide a platform on which a government or political party could campaign. Political proponents of such programs hoped that the opposition would demur, thus providing a convenient election issue. Oppositions frequently failed to take the bait, thus skirting the issue by accepting the program. A patchwork of social programs thus emerged in fits and starts.

Canada ended the war with a limited federal pension program, a universal family allowance scheme, and a housing act designed chiefly to provide employment. In 1945 Ottawa had also proposed to the provinces a national universal pension scheme for Canadians over seventy (with a means test program provincially administered for those sixty-five to sixty-nine), a national public assistance scheme for the unemployed, and a health insurance scheme to be shared by the provinces and the federal government. The almost inevitable demise of the Dominion-Provincial Conference on Reconstruction meant that federal progress on social protection moved ahead extremely slowly. Apart from the creation of the Central Mortgage and Housing Corporation to assist in providing low-cost mortgage loans to Canadian families and a limited home-building program (10,000 houses per year), little happened on the housing front in the fifteen years after 1945. On the health care front, the government in 1948 established a fund for health research and hospital construction, but did little else on health until 1957 when it passed the Hospital Insurance and Diagnostic Services Act. This legislation allowed the federal government to provide 50 per cent of the cost of provincial hospital insurance plans. A new Old Age Security Act of 1951 provided a $40 per month pension to all Canadians over the age of seventy, but still insisted on a means test for those between sixty-five and sixty-nine. In 1956 a limited federal Unemployment Assistance Act with a needs test passed Parliament. Education remained almost entirely a provincial matter before 1960.

In 1945, the last year of the war, federal expenditure was just over $5 billion, with another $451 million spent by the provinces and $250 million by municipalities. In 1960 the Dominion still spent $5 billion, although far less on the military, but provincial governments now spent $2.5 billion and municipalities another $1.7 billion. Much of the increase was on social services. The result was a vast expansion in the number of government employees. In 1945, the last year of the war, the Dominion had 30,240 permanent civil servants and 85,668 temporary ones. At the beginning of 1961, it employed 337,416 Canadians, most of them 'regular' and many of them female. Both provincial and municipal employment grew even faster. The provinces employed 50,000 in 1946 and 257,000 twenty years later, while the municipalities increased from 56,000 in 1946 to 224,000 in 1966. By 1960 there was a sense (on at least the federal level) that matters could get out of hand. . . .

The Expansion of the Welfare State

Part of the reason for the continual expansion of government bureaucracy, of course, was continual (if uncoordinated) expansion of the Canadian welfare state. Politicians viewed expanded social services as popular vote-getters and no political party strenuously opposed the principles of welfare democracy. Although the [John] Diefenbaker government [1957–1963] was not associated with any major program, it had initiated a number of reviews and royal commissions, the recommendations of which would pass into legislation under the Liberals. The minority

THE GROWTH IN SOCIAL SPENDING: 1961–1970

Between 1961 and 1970, as the following chart indicates, Canada's total spending on social security grew from roughly $3.3 billion to $8.7 billion.

Year	Total Social Security Expenditure (in thousands of dollars)
1961	3,287,981
1962	3,541,417
1963	3,824,059
1964	3,997,026
1965	4,378,256
1966	4,674,574
1967	5,380,920
1968	6,664,418
1969	7,620,284
1970	8,719,886

Statistics Canada, www.statcan.ca.

[Lester B.] Pearson government [1963–1968] was pushed towards improved social insurance by the NDP, its own reforming wing, and competitive pressures from an ambitious Quebec and other provinces. Were Ottawa not to introduce new national programs, the federal government could well lose control of them to the wealthier and more aggressive provinces. The expansion in 1964 of family allowances to include children up to the age of eighteen who were still in school merely imitated something introduced by the [Jean] Lesage government [in Quebec] in 1961. In 1965 the federal government attempted to introduce a national contributory pension scheme, settling for one that allowed Quebec its own plan.

The changing demography of Canada guaranteed that there would be continual pressures on the government to improve the pension system. Those who wanted improved benefits were able to make common ground with those who sought to control costs. Both could agree on the superiority of a contributory scheme. The Medical Care Act of 1966 built on provincial initiatives with a cost-sharing arrangement. By 1968 all provinces and territories had agreed on cost-sharing arrangements with Ottawa that produced a social minimum in health care. For most Canadians, access to medical service (doctors and hospitalization) would thereafter be without charge. Occasionally cynicism triumphed. Early in 1965 the prime minister [Lester Pearson] wrote his cabinet ministers asking for suggestions of policy initiatives that would shift attention from political harassment by the opposition over mistakes and difficulties. The result was a Canadian variation of Lyndon Johnson's War on Poverty, which proposed 'a program for the full utilization of our human resources and *the elimination of poverty among our people*'. Actual reforms were not very significant.

The Just Society

The first [Pierre] Trudeau government, responding to the reform euphoria of the era, actually contemplated shifting the grounds of social protectionism in 'the Just Society'. To the late 1960s the emphasis of mainstream reform had been to carry out the agenda of the 1940s for the establishment of a 'social minimum' providing basic economic security for all Canadians. Now, at least briefly, the bureaucrats and politicians debated the possibility of expanding the welfare state to include some measure of income distribution. Poverty became seen as a serious problem worthy of public focus. The Economic Council of Canada in 1968 described the persistence of poverty in Canada as 'a disgrace'. Later that same year a Special Senate Committee on Poverty was established under Senator David Croll's chairmanship. In 1971 this committee produced a report, *Poverty in Canada*, which insisted that nearly 2 million people in Canada lived below the poverty line. More radical critics, in *The Real Poverty Report* that same year, put the figure much higher.

Poverty not only characterized the lives of millions of Canadians, but it was structural, regional, and related to racial and sexual discrimination. A number of schemes were suggested, including guaranteed income for low-income families as part of the family allowance package. The year 1970 had already seen the publication of a federal White Paper called 'Income Security for Canadians', which pointed out the escalating costs of social insurance and criticized the principle of universality that had previously governed Canadian policy. The ultimate result was the new Unemployment Insurance Plan of 1971, which extended and increased coverage without actually confronting the concept of a guaranteed minimum income for all Canadians. At about the same time, Ottawa eliminated a separate fund for Canada pension contributions and began considering them as part of the general revenue of the government.

Reformers had long insisted that access to education was one of the social rights to which all Canadians were entitled. Increasing access meant new facilities. The presence of the baby-boom generation gave urgency to that implication. Parents were much attracted to the practical benefits of education in providing future employment and a better life for their children. The results in the 1960s were enormous pressures on education budgets and increasing demand for the production of more and better teachers. School authorities attempted to ease some of their problems by consolidating rural education through use of the ubiquitous yellow school bus, a process that continued into the early 1970s. Teachers acquired more formal credentials, became better paid, and organized themselves into a powerful professional lobby, sometimes even unionized. By the late 1950s virtually everyone could agree on universal high school education, and by 1970 over 90 per cent of Canadian children of high school age were in school. Increasing numbers of high school graduates were entitled to a university education, and the decade of the 1960s was the golden age of university expansion in Canada. Not only were new facilities constructed but 20,000 new faculty members were recruited, most of them from the United States. By 1970 public spending on education had risen to 9 per cent of the gross national product, and represented nearly 20 per cent of all taxes levied by all three levels of government.

Before 1970 the disagreement between the universalists and the means testers had been relatively muted. Both sides could agree that there had been an absence of overall integrated planning in the growth of the welfare state. Little attention had been paid to the long-range implications of any policy. Bureaucracies and programs had been allowed to expand with no thought for tomorrow. The later 1960s had introduced a new ingredient into the mix, however. Governments began routinely spending more money than they were receiving.

Compassion with Responsibility

By Warren Caragata

In the following piece, first published in 1995 in Maclean's magazine, Canada's major news weekly, Warren Caragata discusses federal cuts to social programs. According to Caragata, Canada's expansive system of social programs was intended to build a benevolent, compassionate, and generous nation. Caragata argues that by the 1990s the Liberal Party, which had been largely responsible for developing these social services, had realized that it was simply costing the country too much. Caragata provides an overview of cuts to federal programs, which, he argues, represent a major reversal for the Liberals. Caragata also notes that most Liberals argue that far from abandoning the goal of a benevolent and caring society, the party has trimmed the budget in order to be able to continue its project in a responsible manner. At the time of writing, Caragata was a senior writer for Maclean's.

It was a time in Canada, in the years following the Second World War, when everything seemed possible. Returning from the battlefields of Europe, the country's best and brightest came to Ottawa to help construct a modern and benevolent land. They would provide seed money for new industries. They would mould a vibrant and unique culture. Above all, they would create a society that was compassionate and generous. Gordon Robertson, who ran the federal bureaucracy as cabinet secretary for prime ministers Lester Pearson and Pierre Trudeau, and who had worked before that for [prime ministers] John Diefenbaker and Louis St. Laurent and Mackenzie King, was one of the architects of that vision. Sitting in his sun-filled study in Ottawa's Rockcliffe district last week, he recalled that hardly anyone was worried about the cost in those days. In fact, he recalled, the only cautionary note about whether the country could actually afford what was being created came from Robert Bryce, then-deputy minister of finance, at a committee meeting of Pearson's cabinet. In the end, "It took about 30 years for Bob Bryce to be proven right," Robertson says.

The final confirmation that Canada cannot afford to be what it aspired to be, came last week. Finance Minister Paul Martin delivered a budget that he declared would finally begin to put Canada's finances in order after decades of rising deficits and national debt. "In this budget," he told sombre MPs [members of parliament] in his budget address, "we are bringing government's size and structure into line with what we can afford." Even for Canadians used to budgets that hurt, Martin's budget was tough: a $25.3-billion cut over three years; 45,000 fewer people on the federal payroll. There will be less money for such once-sacred Liberal totems as social programs, regional development and the Canadian Broadcasting Corporation. Government ownership of Petro-Canada and Canadian National Railway will cease. And even the familiar two-dollar bill will disappear, to be replaced by a coin. Martin also pointed to future revision of pensions, unemployment insurance and cultural agencies. For the upcoming 1995–1996 fiscal year, a combination of $4 billion in cuts and $900 million in tax increases will leave a deficit of $32.7 billion and $24.3 billion the following year. It was, Martin told *Maclean's* in a post-budget interview, a complete rethink of how Ottawa functions.

Cutting Social Programs

It was also a budget that smashed many of the cherished icons of past Liberal governments. That it was Paul Martin Jr. who was doing much of the smashing, however, made it that much more dramatic. As a senior Liberal cabinet minister, his father and namesake worked with Gordon Robertson and the others to construct the welfare state that Martin has now started to dismantle. In his memoirs, *A Very Public Life*, the late Paul Martin recounted his fights with King. "King always considered himself the guardian of the public purse," Martin Sr. grumbled, never thinking that his son might some day feel the same way. But in both his budget speech and his interview with *Maclean's*, Martin insisted that he was, in fact, doing what was necessary to keep his father's legacy alive—protecting social programs from erosion by ever-rising interest payments on the national debt. Interest payments for the 1995–1996 fiscal year, which begins on April 1, will consume $49.5 billion, up from $42 billion this year. That is more than the total spending on pensions, unemployment insurance, health care, welfare and postsecondary education. In fact, that increase in interest payments from this year to next almost matches Ottawa's spending on equalization payments to poorer provinces. "For all of us who care for the social fabric of this country," Martin told the House of Commons, "the state of the nation's finances simply has to be addressed."

Many of those who watched the Liberals attack Conservative Leader Kim Campbell during the 1993 election campaign over her promises to erase the deficit found that turnaround hard to swallow. They include such prominent Liberals as Montreal MP Warren Allmand and Toronto MP Charles Caccia, both of whom were cabinet ministers in the Trudeau era. While Caccia remained grimly silent in public, Allmand took his complaints beyond the closed doors of the Liberal caucus—despite a dressing-down last week from cabinet ministers and fellow MPs. "Some of the measures in the budget are wrong and not in the tradition of the Liberal party," he said. But few other Liberals joined the ranks of the critics, indicating that Martin's budget has widespread—if grudging—support in the caucus. As Manitoba backbencher Marlene Cowling said after Martin spoke in the Commons: "This has been a tough budget, but it had to be done."

A New Path for Liberals

But the budget was more than just a move to bring the federal government closer to its goal of eliminating the deficit. It also marked a continuation of the Liberal party's return to what one strategist called the "pragmatic centre," back to where it sat until the governments of Pierre Trudeau and John Turner. It is a place where Prime Minister Jean Chrétien clearly believes his party should be, a view he has signalled for several years and underscored by his choice of Mitchell Sharp as his mentor and adviser. It was Sharp as finance minister in the Pearson government (with Bryce as his deputy) who advocated a postponement of universal health care until the program could be paid for. The clearest sign of a new path, according to many liberal observers, came not in Martin's budget last week but at a 1991 party conference in Aylmer, Que. "When we form a government," Chrétien said in his remarks opening that session, "we cannot begin from where we left off in 1984."

One indication of how thoroughly Chrétien and Martin have progressed with their renovation of Liberal doctrine was the announcement that all immigrants, including refugees, will be charged a $975 fee for the right to make Canada their home. For a family of four, it will now cost $3,150 to enter Canada. That represents a significant departure in policy for a party that has traditionally relied on the political support of grateful immigrants, who were initially invited to Canada in large numbers by Clifford Sifton, Wilfrid Laurier's interior minister. And the measure plainly outraged immigrant groups, which denounced the new fee structure as the reimposition of the so-called head tax once levied on Asian newcomers.

Another familiar symbol of Liberal economic policy is Petro-Canada, the centrepiece of Ottawa's intervention in the private sector during Trudeau's regime. In 1991, the Progressive Conservatives sold 30 per cent of the company, Canada's second-largest integrated oil company. Now, the Liberals will dispose of the remaining 173 million shares when the market provides a favorable opportunity. The government also plans to shed the Canadian National railway system, nationalized by both Conservative and Liberal administrations after the First World War. Transport Minister Doug Young, an enthusiastic promoter of the new Liberal agenda, said that he hopes the railway, which government officials expect to show a profit of $250 million this year, will be in private hands by year-end.

A key inheritance of past Liberal governments, with pressure from the New Democratic Party and its Co-operative Commonwealth Federation (CCF) forebear, is the country's social safety net. But as much as Martin insists that he is ultimately trying to preserve social programs, that net will become slightly more frayed because of his budget. The biggest change is that, beginning in 1996–1997, federal funding for health care, postsecondary education and welfare will be rolled into something called the Canada Social Transfer, which will come with fewer strings attached. Compared with 1995–1996 levels, the provinces will get $2.5-billion less in the first year of the new transfer and a $4.5-billion reduction in the second year. The provinces cried foul. Saskatchewan Premier Roy Romanow told *Maclean's* that social programs will become an uneven patchwork across the country.

The modification of other social programs is also in the works, including changes to unemployment insurance that the government says will shave a minimum of 10 per cent and save $700 million. But the most potentially controversial step is a reform of the entire pension system slated to take effect in 1997. It was pension reform that deterred the Conservatives from significant social policy changes in their mandate. The Liberals' proposed revision follows the pre-budget release of a report that demonstrated that the Canada Pension Plan will be bankrupt by 2015 unless contribution rates are doubled from current levels.

Romanow has his doubts. The Liberals, he contends, should more clearly define the core goals of the federal government and then cut from there. Still, Romanow, whose government has just introduced a balanced budget, concedes that battles about reinventing the role of government will become much more commonplace in the future. "There is no choice in dealing with the public debt. For me, the politics of the 1990s is the politics of dealing with the debt," he said.

For a long time, Gordon Robertson admits, he thought that Robert Bryce was wrong. He believed—like many others—that Canada's future was so golden that everything was affordable. He has long since changed his mind, although he cannot remember exactly when that shift took place. "It did get beyond what we can afford," he said. "And it isn't a betrayal to go back to what we can afford."

Canada Is Too Liberal

By Stockwell Day

In the following address, Stockwell Day argues that three decades of fiscal and social liberalism have been bad for Canada. As Day sees it, under the Liberal Party of Canada, which dominated Canadian politics since the 1960s, the federal government ballooned in size and ran up huge debts in the name of social welfare. Day argues that although most politicians in Canada have come to recognize the virtues of fiscal responsibility, they remain almost universally socially liberal. Far from seeing such social liberalism as the hallmark of a just society, however, Day argues that it is responsible for widespread social decay. Day criticizes those in Canada who shun and marginalize social and religious conservatives in the name of tolerance. At the time of the address, Day was leader of the Canadian Alliance, a new, right-wing political party.

For the past thirty years, conservative ideas have been considered beyond the pale to many of our self-appointed Canadian elites, the chattering classes, or as British Columbian political commentator Rafe Mair calls them, our "higher purpose persons." According to them, to talk about conservative ideas makes you reactionary, narrow minded, or perhaps even American. But conservatism is deeply rooted in the Canadian tradition. This is a country founded by Conservatives such as John A. Macdonald and George-Etienne Cartier for the profoundly conservative purposes of preserving the British identity of English Canada and the Catholic identity of French Canada.

But many in our chattering classes would have us forget this conservative heritage. Our Canadian elites have been almost monolithically liberal and socialist. For years, the most famous political panel on the CBC [Canadian Broadcasting Corporation] featured the "diverse" views of the socialist Stephen Lewis, the left-leaning Liberal Eric Kierans, and the Red Tory [moderate conservative] Dalton Camp. And while they bickered about the issues of the day, they all agreed that those nutty "neoconservatives," those crazy tax cutters, and dinosaurs like Ted Byfield [a conservative Christian magazine publisher] were a threat to Canada. Being a true conservative was somehow equated with being un-Canadian.

Dalton Camp said recently "anyone who claims to be a Conservative is one. There is no litmus test, no bar to admission, or ban." I beg to differ with Mr. Camp: there is a meaning to the word conservative, and I want to talk about what it means to be conservative today. . . .

Canada's Big Government

The conservative does not rush to use the power of the state to try to radically change economic behaviour or social mores. Rather, the role of government is to pursue a few limited goals and objectives that enable citizens as individuals, families, and communities to achieve their own goals. As Sir John A. Macdonald said, "It is not the place of government to rule, but rather to govern, letting the citizen ebb and flow on the tides of justice and freedom in his own interest, unfettered by unjust laws brought about by hysteria and ignorance."

Since the 1960s, Canada has seen the creation of an ever larger welfare state that wants to rule and micromanage the natural ebb and flow of Canadian society. Today, government controls almost 50 per cent of our Gross Domestic Product. We are taxed to the max, and we are controlled by a maze of suffocating programs and regulations. The good news is that Canadians are starting to say "we have had enough." It is time for a real conservatism in this country, a conservatism that wants to give freedom back to citizens, and return to a government that merely governs, but does not rule our lives.

Now it must be admitted that in recent years, after decades of promoting huge increases in government programs and spending, that a few liberals and even social democrats have begun to twig to the importance of fiscal conservatism.

It is said that a neo-conservative is a liberal who has been mugged by reality. And what we saw happen in Canada in the early 1990s was the tax-and-spend Liberals being mugged by a 200-pound bruiser called the debt wall. Faced with a threat of a devalued currency, massive interest rate hikes, and radical program cuts, the Government of Canada finally in 1995 took the minimum measures necessary to cut the federal deficit. The Liberals became deathbed converts to the virtues of balanced budgets.

They became the beneficiaries of fiscally conservative policies at the provincial level. The effects of reinvigorated economies in Alberta and Ontario, the two provinces reformed by pursuing vigorously conservative principles, helped to fill the federal Liberals' coffers. By skimming revenue from this new growth, by reducing federal transfers to the provinces, and by raising already punishingly high tax rates, they were able to eliminate the deficit. After thirty years of Lester Pearson–Pierre Trudeau–Brian Mulroney economic liberalism, the federal Government discovered, by observing the provinces, that the fiscal conservatism of William Lyon Mackenzie King and Louis St. Laurent had been right all along. . . .

The Problem with Social Liberalism

But while most Canadians, and many of our politicians, admit that the fiscal reforms of the last few years were necessary, we now have a new kind of politician in this country. They are found in all parties, in the New Democratic Party, the Parti Quebecois, the Liberals—at least until the next cabinet shuffle—and the Progressive Conservatives, who say: "I'm fiscally conservative, but I'm socially liberal." Some of these people even argue that this is a libertarian position—that they want government out of both our economic lives and our personal lives. . . .

While many of these politicians have at last grasped fiscal reality, they have not yet awakened to our disintegrating social reality. But they will, and the day they do, many of those fiscal conservatives–but–social liberals will become unhyphenated conservatives. And when they do, they will find a ready home in the Canadian Alliance [a new, fiscally and socially conservative federal party].

Let me tell you why Canada is about to wake up to this social reality. The same undisciplined government spending and social engineering that has undermined our economy over the past thirty years has also been tearing at the social fabric of this land. And while we may not yet have hit the wall, we have built up a social deficit in this country that is every bit as daunting as our fiscal deficit ever was.

Let's look at a few of the facts. Since 1962, violent crimes have increased from about 219 per 100,000 people to over 1000 per 100,000 people—a 500 per cent increase. Divorce has increased from 36 per 10,000 people to 250—a greater than 600 per cent increase. Out of wedlock births have increased from under 5 per cent of childbirths to over 36 per cent of childbirths. The birth-rate has fallen in half, undermining our ability to replace our population. Suicides have almost doubled since the early 1960s and youth suicides—perhaps the canary in the mineshaft of social disintegration—have increased from about 100 per year in 1960 to over 600 per year in the 1990s. From drug addiction to domestic violence, the trends have all been going in the wrong direction. . . .

Liberal Government Is to Blame

We are heading in a disturbing direction in this country, and government, far from helping to solve it, is part of the problem. Our social policies have not adequately supported marriage and have led to an increase in illegitimacy. We have allowed children and adults to think that they can commit crimes with impunity. And a whole generation has been brought up knowing everything about their rights, but rarely hearing about responsibilities.

Liberalism has contributed to the breakdown of our civil society. In the long run it is impossible to maintain a combination of fiscal conservatism and social liberalism because in the long run a socially liberal state, with its incumbent social challenges, is very expensive to maintain. It requires a large welfare state and a costly judicial and police system. A self-governing society with a limited state, by contrast, requires citizens who respect the virtues of family, faith, thrift, civility, and personal responsibility. If we want a limited, fiscally conservative state, then we must nurture and respect the institutions that Edmund Burke called the "little platoons" of civil society—families, small businesses, cultural and faith communities—that give rise to these virtues.

The path we have been pursuing over the past thirty years has not been to promote or respect these institutions, but to undermine them at every turn. The socially liberal state agencies have determined that the Playboy Channel is fine for Canadian airwaves, but a broadcast produced by a crippled, septuagenarian nun named Mother Angelica is a danger to Canada's pluralism and diversity. The socially liberal state funds works of "art" like the pornographic "Bubbles Galore" and documentaries like "The Valour and the Horror" that mock the sacrifices made by Canadians who fought in the Second World War, while neglecting to teach our children about this country's noble history. The socially liberal state has undermined tax benefits to married couples, and penalizes those who raise their children at home while subsidizing out of home daycare. Families should be free to choose the care that meets their needs without the weight of a government reward or punishment system on their shoulders. . . .

Legislating on Morality

Some people actually believe that it is unseemly for politicians to even talk about these kinds of issues. Jeffrey Simpson [a columnist in the *Globe and Mail*, a national newspaper] recently wrote that "Canadians may remain divided on issues such as abortion, capital punishment and homosexuality, but, in the public domain, agreements have been reached on how to handle these issues, either because the courts imposed their will or because legislatures decided some time ago."

Mr. Simpson is right that the courts have imposed their will on some of these issues. We have become all too familiar with judge-made law in this country, and a major debate about the role and scope of judicial review has been underway for some years. In fact, Mr. Simpson has been one of the most eloquent critics of the impact of the Charter [of Rights and Freedoms] in leading to the individualization and fragmentation of Canadian political discourse. . . .

Respect for Religion

Finally, I have to address something that is a deep personal concern of mine. I am a person of religious faith. Like 84 per cent of Canadians, I believe in God. Some people react as though having religious beliefs somehow disqualifies you from holding public office. I would like to ask those who are always accusing religious believers of being intolerant how tolerant they are of people who hold these beliefs.

Let me give but one example of the intolerance shown by some towards those who have strong religious convictions in public life. In 1998, then Progressive Conservative Senator Ron Ghitter delivered a lecture in which he said: "the real threat to the advancement of human rights in Canada today does not come from the skinheads, the Aryan Nation and white supremacists. . . . No, the imminent threat to human rights . . .

comes from what are known as the theo-conservatives."

And who are these people who Mr. Ghitter considers to be more dangerous than neo-Nazis? He named people like Preston Manning [then head of the conservative Reform party], Ted Byfield, Ted Morton [conservative professor of political science at the University of Calgary], and the lobby group REAL Women [a conservative women's group]. They are accused by him of being scolding moralists who seek greater government control over our lives, and pursuing policies which "strike at the very foundations of human rights in Canada." Somehow, I find it hard to take lessons in tolerance from somebody who calls religious conservatives a greater threat to human rights than fascism. . . .

I know that the Canadian people are more tolerant than that, and more tolerant than those in our chattering classes who belittle the religious beliefs of millions of Canadians. Canadians know that the religious beliefs of Catholics, Protestants, Jews, and today of Muslims, Hindus, Sikhs and many others, are what form our deepest convictions. Religious faith is part of what helps keep the social fabric of Canada together, and most Canadians, whether or not they are church goers or religious believers themselves, are at least willing to acknowledge the importance of the religious roots of our society as a force for social good.

The real intolerance in Canadian society is shown by those who would deny people of faith the right to participate in public life. As a social conservative, I honour the communities of religious faith which do so much on a voluntary basis to build families, educate children, feed the hungry, and care for the sick and dying. As a practising Christian within my own faith community, I have been active in some of these areas myself. And I do not believe that a person who has a religious faith is more worthy of democratic and heart-felt respect than someone who is not a person of faith.

The Canadian Military

By Peter C. Newman

The author of the following piece, Peter C. Newman, is a former editor of Maclean's *magazine, Canada's foremost news weekly, and the author of numerous books on Canadian history. In this selection, drawn from his 1983 book* True North: Not Strong and Free, *Newman focuses on the absence of a military tradition in Canada. According to him, although the military is respected and valued in countries such as the United States and the United Kingdom, it has never gripped the public imagination in Canada, despite an impressive record in two world wars. Newman argues that this image of Canada as a "peaceable kingdom" arose, in part, because of Quebec's firm opposition to conscription. Furthermore, he argues, the Canadian view of citizenship does not require its citizens to be patriotic.*

The notion of Canada as a "peaceable kingdom" originated in the writings of Northrop Frye, the greatest of Canada's literary critics. He described an early nineteenth-century painting of that title by Edward Hicks which depicted Indians, Quakers, and animals—lions, bears, oxen, lambs, dogs—all reconciled with one another and the forces of nature. Frye saw in that painting a "haunting vision of serenity" which can also be seen as a recurring theme in Canadian literature.

Throughout Canada's history, we have pursued this quest for a peaceable kingdom. "Canada is an unmilitary community," wrote C.P. Stacey, Canada's pre-eminent military historian, at the beginning of the *Official History of the Canadian Army in the Second World War.* "Warlike her people have often been forced to be, military they have never been." We fought no war of independence, and our home-grown rebellions in Lower and Upper Canada before Confederation hardly qualify as major military actions. We have gone to war as a nation only when allies on other continents were threatened.

After Confederation, the first internal disturbances regarded by the central government as "threats to the state" were [Louis] Riel's Red River Rebellion of 1870 and the Northwest Rebellion of 1884. The latter was important in the context of Prairie settlement and racial tensions of the time, but to call a three-day action at Batoche [a small village in Saskatchewan, site of last conflict of the 1884 rebellion] between adversaries each less than a thousand strong, a "battle," and to label the ten-day containment of a few score of police and civilians in the stockade at [Fort] Battleford [in Saskatchewan] as a "siege," is pure over-dramatization. Other disturbances—the Quebec Conscription Riots of 1917, the Winnipeg General Strike of 1919, and the unemployment marches of the 1930s—may have terrified the governments of the time and indicated political or social crises, but they hardly constituted major military engagements in the history of nations. The most recent threat, the October Crisis of 1970 [in which members of a radical separatist group resorted to kidnapping and murder], caused the government to invoke the War Measures Act in response to an "apprehended insurrection." Seven battalions of regular infantry were mobilized against a group of alleged insurrectionists numbering, according to military analyst John Gellner, "no more than three dozen."

An Impressive Record

Even though we have taken a voluntary hand in defending ourselves ever since 1651, when Pierre Boucher of Trois Rivières formed the beleaguered settlers into our first militia unit, the military mentality has never exercised an important influence in Canadian society. Nonetheless, our military record in overseas wars is second to none in valour and national effort. Between 1914 and 1918, the Canadian army demonstrated courage and sacrifice far beyond the call of duty. At Vimy Ridge, Ypres, Courcelette, Hill 70, the Somme, Passchendaele, and dozens of other battlefields, Canadians endured the hell of trench warfare, suffering an eventual 59,544 casualties. Some 172,950, mostly men, some women, came home wounded, many doomed to spend the rest of their lives in the dreary corridors of veterans' hospitals. Although it received little notice, a fledgling Canadian navy of 9,600 men fought that war too, many of its volunteers serving with the Royal Navy. Uniforms, discipline, and traditions were adopted from Britain's senior service without question or modification, setting the atmosphere of Canada's naval service for generations to come.

Despite Canada's considerable pre-war contribution to the pioneering of flight, no Canadian air force was established, but by the end of 1918, nearly twenty-three thousand Canadians had joined Britain's Royal Flying Corps. Ten of the Royal Air Force's twenty-seven official "aces," including Billy Bishop and Raymond Collishaw, were Canadians, each being credited with thirty or more "kills." After the war, when Canada decided to establish its own air force, it, too, was to be based on the British model, but, in contrast to the navy or the army, Canada didn't simply adopt the ways of the RAF. Since twenty-five per cent of the officers of the original Royal Flying Corps had been Canadian, they had had a good share in creating the joint traditions.

Between the two world wars the Canadian navy, militia, and air force barely managed to survive, but the scale of the Canadian war effort between 1939 and 1945 was awesomely impressive. Canada entered the war two years before the United States. From a population of ten million, more than one million men and women enlisted in our services, an overwhelming number of them volunteers. During the war, forty-two thousand died or were listed as missing. The Royal Canadian Navy, by 1945, was responsible for escorting four-fifths of the Atlantic convoys with a fleet of nearly a thousand destroyers, frigates, corvettes, and miscellaneous craft. The Royal Canadian Air Force contributed forty-five squadrons overseas. The British Commonwealth Air Training Plan produced 131,000 graduates, of whom more than half were Canadian. It was Canada's army that spearheaded the Dieppe raid and fought valiantly during the invasions of Sicily, Italy, and Normandy.

A Lack of Respect

Despite the country's brave record (and eighty-six Victoria Crosses) in both world wars, there has never existed—except perhaps in the private musings of the few staff officers who have bothered to tackle the subject in unpublished essays—any perceived or proclaimed indigenous Canadian military strategy. The country's senior military training establishment, Royal Military College in Kingston, is now 110 years old, and has in the past produced many distinguished graduates in both the military and civilian worlds, but even so, Canadians have found themselves with no lasting heritage in the crafts of war—or even much of an instinct for self-defence. Canadian Legion [veterans'] parades these days draw more marchers than spectators.

The absence of any deep-rooted military tradition in this country is probably the single most important factor preventing any collective push for higher spending on national defence. There is also an absence of respect and interest towards the military on the part of both the public and many of our political leaders, from the top down. During the 1983 provincial election in British Columbia, New Democratic Party Leader David Barrett managed to generate laughs by quipping that "any country that buys submarines that leak and CF-18 airplanes that don't fly can't be all bad." The witticism accurately caught the stereotype of the armed forces in the minds of most Canadians. We tend to think of our military men and women—if we think of them at all—as short-haired amateurs, misfits who couldn't quite make it in civilian life, but who aren't basically warlike or particularly plausible about their profession. Hal Lawrence, one of Canada's Second World War heroes (he was awarded a Distinguished Service Cross for his part in the sinking of the U-94), once summed up this attitude in a letter to me:

> After Admiral H.T.W. Grant had retired as Chief of Naval Staff I was at his home one evening and asked him: "Why is it, sir, that when I'm in the UK and someone asks me what I do and I say I am a Lieutenant in the Royal Canadian Navy, he says, 'Oh, really, jolly good. You must come down for a weekend.' And when I'm asked the same question in the US and give the same reply, I'm told, 'Oh, good, you must come out and meet the little woman.'
>
> "But when the same question and answer are exchanged in Canada, there's an awkward pause while everyone thinks: 'Poor fellow. Probably didn't do well in Grade 12.'"
>
> "My dear Lawrence," the Admiral replied, "it has always been thus. In the UK, everyone knows the Navy and that it has kept them free for centuries; it doesn't matter if it's true or not. In the US, the military threw

off the oppression of a distant tyrant and sailors have
kept the tyrant out ever since. Again, it's not as simple
as that, but that's what everyone believes. In Canada, on
the other hand, we have always fought distant wars: in
Egypt in the last century, in South Africa at the turn of
the century, in Europe in 1914–18, in Europe, North
Africa, and the Far East in 1939–45."

"But what about the attack on Quebec by the Americans? What about the land and sea battles of 1812–14?
What about our ships being sunk close to Quebec in
1939–45?"

"Few people know about that and fewer care. Have another glass of port and calm down."

Apart from the Mainstream

The military in this country operate outside the mainstream of
society. Writing in the *Canadian Defence Quarterly*, two officers,
Major-General Loomis and Lieutenant-Colonel Lightburn, recently took this argument in another direction, observing that military society in Canada has been set apart by its resemblance to a
"secular religion." They stated that "an attempt has been made to
integrate our military sub-culture into the main body of Canadian society: the sharp-toothed guard dog has been taken into the
home to be made a family pet." This is a dubious proposition,
since family pets, no matter how toothless, enjoy a playful fond-
ness hardly accorded this country's armed forces, which have sel-
dom attracted any public sentiment kinder than benign neglect.
This has been true even at the highest level of Canadian politics.
In his book, *Ministers and Generals*, Professor Desmond Morton
documents at least two instances in earlier years when Canadian
prime ministers have voiced the thoughts that Canada had no real
need for defence forces of its own and that defence expenditures
were really just another tool of the political reward system.

The use of our armed forces to support political, external, and
industrial policies without the actual military requirements first being taken into account has been standard practice throughout
Canadian history. Our political leaders have demonstrated an as-
tonishing lack of confidence in their own military advisors. Writing about the War Committee of his own Cabinet at the height
of the 1939–45 conflict, Prime Minister Mackenzie King confided

to his diary: "I ruled out having the Canadian Chiefs of Staff present. It had been [Arnold] Heeney [then civilian secretary to the Cabinet] who had arranged for these meetings himself, as he said, just to give the Chiefs of Staff a 'look in' and let them feel important. The proceedings made it apparent that they were not needed and, by their not being present, the discussions were shortened."

It was not *because of* the country's political leadership, but *despite* it, that Canadians achieved such enviable reputations in two world wars.

In fact, our political history seems to indicate that we have a positive reluctance to choose a prime minister with any military associations. None of Canada's sixteen prime ministers have had significant senior military experience. (Curiously, the one with the most wartime service was Nobel Peace Prize winner Lester Pearson, who served for a time in the First World War as a junior officer, and who also had the closest personal associations with senior military officers.)

Canadians do not have the tradition of universal or compulsory military service that has been the experience of citizens of the United States, the United Kingdom, or for that matter, the Soviet Republics. For inescapable political reasons ours is an all-volunteer system, and even at the height of wartime emergencies, it has proved to be virtually impossible to introduce conscription.

During both world wars there was some resistance to compulsory military service in rural areas and in the labour movement throughout Canada, but the real opposition came from Quebec. Despite the distinguished military record of many French Canadians, Quebec has always been politically firm on this issue. During the First World War the Borden government, desperate for troop reinforcements for the trenches, initiated a move for conscription. The result was riots in Montreal and an absolute political rift between Quebec and the rest of Canada. Again, in the latter years of the Second World War, Mackenzie King, with his notorious phrase "conscription if necessary, but not necessarily conscription," attempted to provide conscripted support for overseas forces. Once again that implacable opposition to conscription occurred in Quebec. Quebec's recent history of enthusiastic support for René Lévesque [the Quebec separatist], if not for all of his policies, suggests that there would be an equally strong refusal today to compulsory service in Canada's armed forces, regardless of the threat to national security.

A Different View of Citizenship

The lack of relevance under which our professional military must operate flows from one of Canadian society's deepest-rooted convictions: that we are a cultural free port, a society so open that our citizens need claim no loyalties, not even a belief in their own country. In his introduction to *Canada: A Landscape Portrait*, Robert Fulford, the editor of *Saturday Night*, spotlighted this attitude by describing the differences noted by American draft dodgers who came here during the Vietnam War.

> What they noticed first about Canada was the absence of a compulsion to conform. They discovered to their surprise that patriotism is not a prerequisite of Canadian citizenship. What the draft dodgers found in Canada was a unique kind of psychic freedom, a rather different matter from political freedom. It is this freedom, expressed in ethnic, linguistic, and regional terms, that forms the real basis of Canadian life.
>
> The curious fact is that, in order to qualify as Canadians, we are not required to be loyal, even in theory, to the idea of Canada. At an editorial meeting at *Maclean's* [a major news weekly] early in the 1960s, the then-new subject of Quebec separatism was introduced. One editor declared firmly that separatists should be prosecuted for treason. He was an English immigrant, still innocent in Canadian ways, and his suggestion was greeted with derisive laughter, but it occurred to me at the time that if one looked at his views from a global perspective they were not altogether preposterous. In a very few countries would the idea of national dismemberment be greeted with such insouciance. But in fact, by unspoken agreement, Canadian citizenship carries the ultimate freedom: the freedom to declare that one doesn't want to be Canadian, to urge that one's region should cease to be part of Canada, and yet to go on being a Canadian and receiving the appropriate benefits.

This notion—that "patriotism is not a prerequisite of Canadian citizenship"—is one of the fundamental differences between Americans and Canadians. It pervades everything that we are, do, and hope to become.

Multiculturalism and the Future of Canada

The Canadian Multiculturalism Act

BY THE GOVERNMENT OF CANADA

The Canadian Multiculturalism Act of 1988 extended and strengthened the federal government's role in promoting multiculturalism, a policy it first adopted in 1971. The following excerpt from the act outlines the government's goals and strategies for achieving those goals. In particular, the government pledges to actively support cultural diversity by helping preserve the use of languages other than English and French and by supporting projects, programs, and organizations that work to recognize and preserve cultural diversity.

WHEREAS the Constitution of Canada provides that every individual is equal before and under the law and has the right to the equal protection and benefit of the law without discrimination and that everyone has the freedom of conscience, religion, thought, belief, opinion, expression, peaceful assembly and association and guarantees those rights and freedoms equally to male and female persons;

AND WHEREAS the Constitution of Canada recognizes the importance of preserving and enhancing the multicultural heritage of Canadians;

AND WHEREAS the Constitution of Canada recognizes rights of the aboriginal peoples of Canada;

AND WHEREAS the Constitution of Canada and the *Official Languages Act* provide that English and French are the official languages of Canada and neither abrogates nor derogates from any rights or privileges acquired or enjoyed with respect to any other language;

The Government of Canada, "The Canadian Multiculturalism Act. R.S., 1985, c. 24 (4th Supp.), Bill C-18-7, assented to July 21, 1988," www.pch.gc.ca, July 21, 1988.

AND WHEREAS the *Citizenship Act* provides that all Canadians, whether by birth or by choice, enjoy equal status, are entitled to the same rights, powers and privileges and are subject to the same obligations, duties and liabilities;

AND WHEREAS the *Canadian Human Rights Act* provides that every individual should have an equal opportunity with other individuals to make the life that the individual is able and wishes to have, consistent with the duties and obligations of that individual as a member of society, and, in order to secure that opportunity, establishes the Canadian Human Rights Commission to redress any proscribed discrimination, including discrimination on the basis of race, national or ethnic origin or colour;

AND WHEREAS Canada is a party to the *International Convention on the Elimination of All Forms of Racial Discrimination*, which Convention recognizes that all human beings are equal before the law and are entitled to equal protection of the law against any discrimination and against any incitement to discrimination, and to the *International Covenant on Civil and Political Rights*, which Covenant provides that persons belonging to ethnic, religious or linguistic minorities shall not be denied the right to enjoy their own culture, to profess and practise their own religion or to use their own language;

AND WHEREAS the Government of Canada recognizes the diversity of Canadians as regards race, national or ethnic origin, colour and religion as a fundamental characteristic of Canadian society and is committed to a policy of multiculturalism designed to preserve and enhance the multicultural heritage of Canadians while working to achieve the equality of all Canadians in the economic, social, cultural and political life of Canada;

NOW, THEREFORE, Her Majesty, by and with the advice and consent of the Senate and House of Commons of Canada, enacts as follows: . . .

The Multiculturalism Policy

3. (1) It is hereby declared to be the policy of the Government of Canada to

(a) recognize and promote the understanding that multiculturalism reflects the cultural and racial diversity of Canadian society and acknowledges the freedom of all members of Canadian society to preserve, enhance and share their cultural heritage;

(b) recognize and promote the understanding that multicul-

turalism is a fundamental characteristic of the Canadian heritage
and identity and that it provides an invaluable resource in the
shaping of Canada's future;

(c) promote the full and equitable participation of individuals
and communities of all origins in the continuing evolution and
shaping of all aspects of Canadian society and assist them in the
elimination of any barrier to that participation;

(d) recognize the existence of communities whose members
share a common origin and their historic contribution to Canadian society, and enhance their development;

(e) ensure that all individuals receive equal treatment and equal
protection under the law, while respecting and valuing their
diversity;

(f) encourage and assist the social, cultural, economic and political institutions of Canada to be both respectful and inclusive
of Canada's multicultural character;

(g) promote the understanding and creativity that arise from
the interaction between individuals and communities of different origins;

(h) foster the recognition and appreciation of the diverse cultures of Canadian society and promote the reflection and the
evolving expressions of those cultures;

(i) preserve and enhance the use of languages other than English and French, while strengthening the status and use of the
official languages of Canada; and

(j) advance multiculturalism throughout Canada in harmony
with the national commitment to the official languages of
Canada. . . .

Preserving Diversity

5. (1) The [Multiculturalism] Minister shall take such measures as
the Minister considers appropriate to implement the multiculturalism policy of Canada and, without limiting the generality of
the foregoing, may

(a) encourage and assist individuals, organizations and institutions to project the multicultural reality of Canada in their activities in Canada and abroad;

(b) undertake and assist research relating to Canadian multiculturalism and foster scholarship in the field;

(c) encourage and promote exchanges and cooperation among
the diverse communities of Canada;

(d) encourage and assist the business community, labour organizations, voluntary and other private organizations, as well as public institutions, in ensuring full participation in Canadian society, including the social and economic aspects, of individuals of all origins and their communities, and in promoting respect and appreciation for the multicultural reality of Canada;

(e) encourage the preservation, enhancement, sharing and evolving expression of the multicultural heritage of Canada;

(f) facilitate the acquisition, retention and use of all languages that contribute to the multicultural heritage of Canada;

(g) assist ethno-cultural minority communities to conduct activities with a view to overcoming any discriminatory barrier and, in particular, discrimination based on race or national or ethnic origin; [and]

(h) provide support to individuals, groups or organizations for the purpose of preserving, enhancing and promoting multiculturalism in Canada.

The Perils of Multiculturalism

By Neil Bissoondath

The author of the following article, Neil Bissoondath, is a writer and out-spoken critic of Canada's multiculturalism policy. Bissoondath, who immigrated to Canada from Trinidad in 1973, argues that although Canadian policy purports to preserve the distinct cultures of immigrants, it actually devalues those cultures by promoting simplified, superficial visions of them. As Bissoondath sees it, multiculturalism threatens to divide Canadians. He argues that immigrants under the multicultural policy often remain more committed to their country of birth than to Canada. This, he believes, threatens the value of Canadian citizenship and democracy.

The consequences of multiculturalism policy are many and varied, but none is as ironic—or as unintended—as what I would call the simplification of culture.

The public face of Canadian multiculturalism is flashy and attractive, emerging with verve and gaiety from the bland stereotype of traditional Canada at festivals around the country. At Toronto's "Caravan," for instance, various ethnic groups rent halls in churches or community centres to create "pavilions" to which access is gained through an ersatz passport. Once admitted—passport duly stamped with a "visa"—you consume a plate of Old World food at distinctly New World prices, take a quick tour of the "craft" and "historical" displays, then find a seat for the "cultural" show, traditional songs (often about wheat) and traditional dances (often about harvesting wheat) performed by youths resplendent in their traditional costumes.

After the show, positively glowing with your exposure to yet another slice of our multicultural heritage, you make your way to the next pavilion, to the next line up for food, the next dis-

Neil Bissoondath, "A Question of Belonging: Multiculturalism and Citizenship," *The Meaning and Future of Canadian Citizenship*, edited by William Kaplan. Montreal: McGill-Queen's University Press, 1993. Copyright © 1993 by McGill-Queen's University Press. Reproduced by permission.

play, the next bout of cultural edification. At the end of the day, you may be forgiven if you feel you have just spent several long hours at a folksy Disneyland with multicultural versions of Mickey, Minnie, and Goofy.

This in fact is all you have really done. Your exposure has been not to culture but to theatre, not to history but to fantasy: enjoyable, no doubt, but of questionable significance. You come away knowing nothing of the language and literature of these places, little of their past and their present—and what you have seen is usually shaped with blatantly political ends in mind. You have acquired no sense of the everyday lives—the culture—of the people in these places, but there is no doubt that they are each and every one open, sincere, and fun-loving.

Such displays are uniquely suited to seeking out the lowest common denominator. Comfortable only with superficialities, they reduce cultures hundreds, sometimes thousands, of years old to easily digested stereotypes. One's sense of Ukrainian culture is restricted to perogies and Cossack dancing: Greeks, we learn, are all jolly Zorbas, and Spaniards dance flamenco between bouts of "Viva España"; Germans gulp beer, sauerkraut, and sausages while belting out Bavarian drinking songs; Italians make good ice-cream, great coffee, and all have connections to shady godfathers. And the Chinese continue to be a people who form conga lines under dragon costumes and serve good, cheap food in slightly dingy restaurants.

Devaluing Culture

Our approach to multiculturalism thus encourages the devaluation of that which it claims to wish to protect and promote. Culture becomes an object for display rather than the heart and soul of the individuals formed by it. Culture, manipulated into social and political usefulness, becomes folklore—as [Quebec politician René] Lévesque said—lightened and simplified, stripped of the weight of the past. None of the cultures that make up our "mosaic" seems to have produced history worthy of exploration or philosophy worthy of consideration.

I am reminded of the man who once said to me that he would never move into an apartment building that housed any East Indian families because the building was sure to be infested with roaches: East Indians, he explained, view cockroaches as creatures of good luck, and they give live ones as gifts to each other. I had known the man for some time, was certain that he was in no way racist—a perception confirmed by the fact that he was admitting this to me, someone clearly of East Indian descent. His hesitation was not racial but cultural. I was not of India: he would not hesitate in having me for a neighbour. So searching for an apartment, he perceived the neighbours not as fellow Canadians old or new but as cockroach-lovers, a "cultural truth" that he had accepted without question. But what would he have done, I wondered later with some discomfort, had he seen me emerging from a building that he was about to visit?

The vision that many of us have of each other is one of division. It is informed by misunderstanding and misconception: what we know of each other is often at best superficial, at worst malicious. And multiculturalism, with all of its festivals and its celebrations, has done nothing to foster a factual and clear-headed vision of the other. Depending on stereotype, ensuring that ethnic groups will preserve their distinctiveness in a gentle form of cultural apartheid, multiculturalism has done little but lead an already divided country down the path to further social divisiveness. . . .

The Limits of Multiculturalism

In the West Indies long and boisterous parties, on the whole, inconvenience no one. They are held at houses, both inside and outside. Neighbours tend to be invited, children sleep where they fall. Food and drink are in plentiful supply, music is loud and lively, meant not as background filler but as foreground incentive to dance. There is nothing sedate about the archetypal West Indian party. So central is "a good time" to the West Indian sense of self that someone—not a West Indian—once wryly commented that she had the impression that parties, and not calypso or reggae, were the great West Indian contribution to world culture. Booming music, the yelp and rumble of excited voices, the tramp of dancing feet are accepted as an integral part of the region's cultural life.

Transfer this to, say, Toronto—not to a house surrounded by an extensive yard but to an apartment hemmed in by other apartments. Transfer the music, the dancing, the shouting—everything but the fact that the neighbours, here unknown and uncommunicative, are not likely to be invited. It takes little imagination to appreciate the tensions that may, and do, arise.

A simple lack of consideration for the rights of others? Yes—

but it may be, as some claim, that everything is political. The view has been expressed to me more than once that, in view of the importance of parties in West Indian culture, and considering the official policy of multicultural preservation in Canada, complaints about noise or demands that stereo volumes be lowered can be viewed as a form of cultural aggression. Changing the tone of the party, the argument goes, results in a lessening of its Caribbean character—and is therefore a sign of cultural intolerance. Implicit in this view is the idea that everything deemed cultural is sacred—as well as the idea that the surrounding society must fully accommodate itself to displays, no matter how disruptive, of cultural life. In this atmosphere, a party is no longer just a party; it becomes a form of cultural expression and therefore a subject of political and legal protection.

This is an admittedly aggressive interpretation of the workings of multicultural policy, but it is neither farfetched nor fully indefensible. Open-ended political policy is, almost without exception, subject to an endless stretching of the envelope: there will always be someone—or some group—attempting to go farther than anyone else has gone before.

The Multiculturalism Act suggests no limits to the accommodation offered to different ethnic practices, so that a Muslim group in Toronto recently demanded, in the name of respect for its culture, the right to opt out of the Canadian judicial system in favour of Islamic law, a body of thought fundamental to the life and cultural outlook of its practising members. In the opinion of its spokesmen, this right should be a given in a truly multicultural society.

A Divided Culture

More recently, the Ontario College of Physicians and Surgeons expressed concern over a rise, unexplained and unexpected, in the number of requests for female circumcision. According to a report in the *Toronto Star* on 6 January 1992, the procedure, long viewed in Western culture as a kind of mutilation, involves "cutting off a young girl's external genital parts, including the clitoris. In some countries, it includes stitching closed the vulva until marriage, leaving a small opening for urination and menstrual flow. . . . Various health risks have been linked to it, including immediate serious bleeding, recurring infections, pain during intercourse, hemorrhaging during childbirth and infertility. . . . Charles

Kayzze, head of Ottawa's African Resource Centre, believes it is being performed here by members of the community. In some cases, he says, families are sending their children to Africa to have it done." The result is the reduction of the woman to the status of machine, capable of production but mechanically, with no pleasure in the process.

It is curious that such ideas can be brought to this land, survive, and then present a problem to doctors for whom policy guidelines, never before necessary, are now being established. ("The policy," the report states, "is likely to say Ontario doctors should not perform the operation.") Yet one awaits with bated breath calls for public performance of the ancient Hindu rite of suttee in which widows are cremated alive on their husband's funeral pyres.

There is a certain logic to all of this, but a logic that indicates a certain disdain for the legal and ethical values that shape, and are shaped by, Canadian society—and therefore for Canadian society itself.

And why not, given that the picture that the country transmits of itself is one that appears to diminish a unified whole in favour of an ever-fraying mosaic? If Canada, as a historical, social, legal, and cultural concept, does not demand respect, why should respect be expected? . . .

Citizenship and Loyalty

The reasons for taking that final step toward full citizenship are many and varied. They emerge from the realization that all of one's intellectual and emotional loyalties have come, through the years, to commit themselves to Canada. One makes a life, puts down roots. And from this feeling of belonging comes the wish to be as fully part of the country as possible.

However, the diminishing value of Canadian citizenship—the creation of the hyphenated Canadian with divided loyalties, the perception that immigration policy now allows the rich to buy their way into the country, the idea that citizenship is a natural right and not an earned privilege—means that the exact opposite has also come to be true. The acquisition of Canadian citizenship is frequently seen not as a means of committing oneself to the country but as a way of leaving it with an assurance of safety.

Few passports are safer than a Canadian one, and for many people citizenship implies merely access to a passport that allows return to the comforts of the former homeland with the assurance of safe haven should plans go awry, or should political instability necessitate flight. There is no way to prevent this, and those who wish to acquire only a passport of convenience enjoy the right. But the implications for the country cannot be ignored. I would suggest that any country that does not claim the full loyalty of its citizens old or new, any country that counts citizens old or new who treat it as they would a public washroom—that is, as merely a place to run to in an emergency—accepts for itself a severe internal weakening. It is perhaps inevitable that for many newcomers Canada is merely a job. It is desperately sad, though, when, after many years, they see Canada as only that. Multiculturalism, with its emphasis on the importance of holding on to the former homeland, with its insistence that *There* is more important than *Here*, serves to encourage this attitude.

In a democracy, any legislation to address such a problem must be viewed as anathema, for it cannot help but be a gesture of tyranny. So although there is no role here for the legislator, there is a vital role for the policy-maker. Multiculturalism, if it is in fact aimed at shaping Canadian society in a cohesive way, should seek out policies that would encourage engagement with the society rather than exploitation of it. From this point of view, multiculturalism has served us badly. . . .

Canada has long prided itself on being a tolerant society, but tolerance is clearly insufficient in the building of a cohesive society. A far greater goal to strive for would be an *accepting* society. Multiculturalism seems to offer at best provisional acceptance, and it is with some difficulty that one insists on being a full—and not just an associate—member. Just as the newcomer must decide how best to accommodate himself or herself to the society, so the society must in turn decide how it will accommodate itself to the newcomer. Multiculturalism has served neither interest; it has highlighted our differences rather than diminished them, has heightened division rather than encouraged union. More than anything else, the policy has led to the institutionalization and enhancement of a ghetto mentality. And it is here that lies the multicultural problem as we experience it in Canada: a divisiveness so entrenched that we face a future of multiple solitudes with no central notion to bind us.

The Merits of Multiculturalism

By WILL KYMLICKA

Will Kymlicka, a professor at Queen's University in Kingston, Ontario, is the author of numerous books on political philosophy, democracy, citizenship, and ethnocultural diversity. In this selection, Kymlicka argues that those who criticize Canada's multicultural policy on the grounds that it encourages ethnic divisiveness are mistaken on the facts. The Canadian model, he argues, has been far more successful than the approaches favored in the United States and Europe. According to Kymlicka, immigrants to Canada are able to both preserve their ethnic identity and successfully integrate into Canadian society.

In 1971, Canada embarked on a unique experiment by declaring a policy of official "multiculturalism". According to [Prime Minister] Pierre Trudeau, who introduced it in the House of Commons, the policy had the following four aims: to support the cultural development of ethnocultural groups; to help members of ethnocultural groups to overcome barriers to full participation in Canadian society; to promote creative encounters and interchange among all ethnocultural groups; and to assist new Canadians in acquiring at least one of Canada's official languages.

Although the policy of multiculturalism was first adopted by the federal government, it was explicitly designed as a model for other levels of government, and indeed it has been copied widely. "Multiculturalism programs" can now be found, not just in the multiculturalism office of the federal government, but also at the provincial or municipal levels of government, and indeed within a wide range of public and private institutions, such as schools or businesses.

These policies are now under attack, more so today than at any time since 1971. And perhaps it is time for a re-evaluation. We

Will Kymlicka, "The Theory and Practice of Canadian Multiculturalism," *A Presentation to Breakfast on the Hill, Ottawa, November 24, 1998.* Kingston, Ontario: Will Kymlicka, 1998. Copyright © 1998 by Will Kymlicka. Reproduced by permission.

now have over twenty-five years of experience of multicultur-alism, and the time has come to step back and examine whether the policy has served its intended goals, and whether it still has a useful function to play in today's world. . . .

The Impact of Multiculturalism

The debate over multiculturalism has heated up in recent years, largely because of two recent best selling critiques of the pol-icy—Neil Bissoondath's *Selling Illusions: The Cult of Multicultural-ism in Canada* (1994), and Richard Gwyn's *Nationalism Without Walls: The Unbearable Lightness of Being Canadian* (1995). Both Bis-soondath and Gwyn make very similar claims about the results of the policy. In particular, both argue that multiculturalism has pro-moted a form of ethnic separatism amongst immigrants. Thus Bissoondath says that multiculturalism has led to "undeniable ghettoization". Rather than promoting integration, multicultur-alism is encouraging the idea that immigrants should form "self-contained" ghettos "alienated from the mainstream". This ghet-toization is "not an extreme of multiculturalism but its ideal: a way of life transported whole, a little outpost of exoticism pre-served and protected". He approvingly quotes Arthur Schles-inger's claim that multiculturalism rests upon a "cult of ethnic-ity" which "exaggerates differences, intensifies resentments and antagonisms, drives even deeper the awful wedges between races and nationalities. The endgame is self-pity and self-ghettoization", or what Schlesinger calls "cultural and linguistic apartheid". Ac-cording to Bissoondath, multiculturalism policy does not en-courage immigrants to think of themselves as Canadians, and in-deed even the children of immigrants "continue to see Canada with the eyes of foreigners. Multiculturalism, with its emphasis on the importance of holding on to the former or ancestral homeland, with its insistence that *There* is more important than *Here*, encourages such attitudes".

Gwyn makes the same claim, in very similar language. He ar-gues that "official multiculturalism encourages apartheid, or to be a bit less harsh, ghettoism". The longer multiculturalism pol-icy has been in place, "the higher the cultural walls have gone up inside Canada". Multiculturalism encourages ethnic leaders to keep their members "apart from the mainstream", practising "what can best be described as mono-culturalism". In this way, "Our state encourages these gatekeepers to maintain what amounts, at worst, to an apartheid form of citizenship".

Bissoondath and Gwyn are hardly alone in these claims—they are repeated endlessly in the media. To take just one more example, Robert Fulford recently argued in the *Globe and Mail* that the policy encourages people to maintain their identity "freeze-dried", and hence reduces intercultural exchange and relationships, and that time will judge it to be one of Canada's greatest "policy failures".

In my view, it is important—indeed urgent—to determine whether this claim is true. Since neither Bissoondath nor Gwyn provide any empirical evidence for their claims, I have tried to collect together some statistics which might bear on the question of whether multiculturalism has promoted ethnic separatism, and discouraged or impeded integration. I will start with evidence from within Canada, comparing ethnic groups before and after the adoption of the multiculturalism policy in 1971. I will then consider comparative evidence, to see how Canada compares with other countries, particularly those countries which have rejected the principle of official multiculturalism.

Integration in Canada

How has the adoption of multiculturalism in 1971 affected the integration of ethnic groups in Canada? To answer this question requires some account of what "integration" involves. It is one of the puzzling features of the Gwyn/Bissoondath critique that they do not define exactly what they mean by integration. However, we can piece together some of the things which they see as crucial ingredients of integration: adopting a Canadian identity, rather than clinging exclusively to one's ancestral identity; participating in broader Canadian institutions, rather than participating solely in ethnic-specific institutions; learning an official language, rather than relying solely on one's mother tongue; having inter-ethnic friendships or even mixed marriages, rather than socializing entirely within one's ethnic group. These sorts of criteria do not form a comprehensive theory of "integration", but they seem to be at the heart of Gwyn and Bissoondath's concerns about multiculturalism, so they are a good starting-point.

Let us begin with the most basic form of integration—namely, the decision of immigrants to become Canadian citizens. If the Gwyn/Bissoondath thesis were true, one would expect naturalization rates to have declined since the adoption of multiculturalism. In fact, however, naturalization rates have increased since 1971. This is particularly relevant since the economic incentives to naturalize have lessened over the last 25 years. Taking out Canadian citizenship is not needed to gain access to the labour market in Canada, or to have access to social benefits. There are virtually no differences between citizens and permanent residents in their civil rights or social benefits—the right to vote is the only major legal benefit gained by naturalization. The primary reason for immigrants to take out citizenship, therefore, is that they identify with Canada; they want to formalize their membership in Canadian society, and participate in the political life of the country.

Moreover, if we examine which groups are most likely to naturalize, we find that it is the "multicultural groups"—that is, immigrants from non-traditional source countries, for whom the multiculturalism policy is most relevant—which have the highest rate of naturalization. By contrast, immigrants from the United States and United Kingdom—who are not seen in popular discourse as an "ethnic" or "multicultural" group—have the lowest rate of naturalization. In other words, those groups which fall most clearly under the multiculturalism policy have shown the greatest desire to become Canadian, while those groups which fall outside the multiculturalism rubric have shown the least desire to become Canadian.

Let's move now to political participation. If the Gwyn/Bissoondath thesis were true, one would expect the political participation of ethnocultural minorities to have declined since the adoption of multiculturalism in 1971. After all, political participation is a symbolic affirmation of citizenship, and reflects an interest in the political life of the larger society. In fact, however, there is no evidence for this claim. To take one relevant indicator, in the period prior to the adoption of multiculturalism between Confederation and the 1960s ethnic groups became increasingly underrepresented in Parliament, but since 1971 the trend has been reversed, so that today they have close to as many MPs as one would expect based on their percentage of the population.

Moreover, it is important to note the way ethnocultural groups participate in Canadian politics. They do not form separate ethnic-based parties, either on a group-by-group basis or even on a coalition basis. Instead, they participate overwhelmingly within pan-Canadian parties. Indeed, the two parties in Canada which are closest to being ethnic parties were created by and for those of English or French ancestry—namely, the Parti/Bloc Québécois, whose support is overwhelmingly found amongst Quebecers with French ancestry, and the Confederation of Regions Party, whose supporters were almost exclusively of English-Loyalist background. By contrast, immigrants have shown no inclination to support ethnic-based political parties, and instead vote for the traditional national parties.

Active, Committed Citizens

This is just one indicator of a more general point—namely, that immigrants are overwhelmingly supportive of, and committed to protecting, the basic political structure in Canada. We know that, were it not for the "ethnic vote", the 1995 referendum on secession in Quebec would have succeeded. In that referendum, ethnics overwhelmingly expressed their commitment to Canada. More generally, all the indicators suggest that immigrants quickly absorb and accept Canada's basic liberal-democratic values and constitutional principles, even if they came from countries which are illiberal or nondemocratic. As Freda Hawkins puts it, "the truth is that there have been no riots, no breakaway political parties, no charismatic immigrant leaders, no real militancy in international causes, no internal political terrorism . . . immigrants recognize a good, stable political system when they see one".

In short, if we look at indicators of legal and political integration, we see that since the adoption of multiculturalism in 1971 immigrants are more likely to become Canadians, and more likely to participate politically. And when they do participate, they do so through pan-ethnic political parties which uphold Canada's basic liberal democratic principles.

This sort of political integration is the main aim of a democratic state. But from the point of view of individual Canadians, the most important form of integration of immigrants is probably not political, but linguistic and social. Immigrants who participate in politics may be good democratic citizens, but if they can't speak English or French, or are socially isolated in self-contained ethnic groups, then Canadians will perceive a failure of integration. So let us shift now to two indicators of societal integration, namely, official language acquisition and intermarriage rates.

If the Gwyn/Bissoondath thesis were true, one would expect the desire of ethnocultural minorities to acquire official language

competence to have declined since the adoption of multiculturalism in 1971. If immigrant groups are being "ghettoized",
"alienated from the mainstream", attempting to preserve their
original way of life intact from their homeland, then presumably
they have less reason to learn an official language.

In fact, however, demand for English as a Second Language
and French as a Second Language classes has never been higher,
and indeed exceeds supply in many cities. Recent census statistics show that 98.6% of Canadians say that they can speak one of
the official languages. This is a staggering statistic when one considers how many immigrants are elderly and/or illiterate in their
mother-tongue, and who therefore find it extremely difficult to
learn a new language. It is especially impressive given that the
number of immigrants who arrive with knowledge of an official language has declined since 1971. If we set aside the elderly—who form the majority of Canadians who cannot speak
an official language—the idea that there is a general decrease in
immigrants' desire to learn an official language is absurd. Immigrants want to learn an official language, and the overwhelming
majority do so. Insofar as their official language skills are lacking,
the explanation is the lack of accessible and appropriate language
classes, not the lack of desire.

Social Integration

One final indicator worth looking at is intermarriage rates. If the
Gwyn/Bissoondath thesis were true, one would expect intermarriage rates to have declined since the adoption of multiculturalism, since the policy is said to have driven "even deeper the
awful wedges between races and nationalities", and encouraged
groups to retreat into their "monocultural" ghettos, and hide behind "cultural walls".

In fact, however, intermarriage rates have consistently increased
since 1971. There has been an overall decline in endogamy [mar-
riage within a particular group] both for immigrants and their
native-born children. Moreover, and equally importantly, we see
a dramatic increase in social acceptance of mixed marriages. For
example, whereas 52% of Canadians disapproved of black-white
marriages in 1968, 81% approved of them in 1995.

Unlike the previous three indicators of integration, intermarriage is not a deliberate goal of government policy. Governments should neither encourage nor discourage intermarriage.

But changes in the rate of intermarriage are useful, I think, as an indicator of a broader trend which is a legitimate government concern—namely, the extent to which Canadians feel comfortable living and interacting with members of other ethnic groups. If Canadians feel comfortable living and working with members of other groups, the inevitable result is that some people will become friends with, and even lovers of, those from other ethnic groups. The fact that intermarriage rates have gone up is important, therefore, not necessarily in and of itself, but rather as evidence that Canadians are more accepting of diversity. And indeed we have direct evidence for this more general trend. Canadians today are much more accepting of having members of other ethnic groups as coworkers, neighbours, or friends than they were before 1971.

If we examined other indicators, we would get the same story. For example, despite Gywn and Bissoondath's rhetoric about the proliferation of ethnic "ghettos" and "enclaves", studies of residential concentration have shown that the phenomenon of permanent ethnic enclaves is nonexistent in Canada. Indeed, "it is scarcely sensible to talk of 'ghettos' in Canadian cities". Moreover, what little concentration does exist is more likely to be found in older immigrant groups, like the Jews and Italians, who preceded the multiculturalism policy. Those groups which have primarily arrived after 1971, such as Asians and Afro-Caribbeans, exhibit the least residential concentration.

In short, whether we look at naturalization, political participation, official language competence, or intermarriage rates, we see the same story. There is no evidence to support the claim that multiculturalism has decreased the rate of integration of immigrants, or increased the separatism or mutual hostility of ethnic groups.

Canada in Comparison

We can make the same point another way. If the Bissoondath/Gwyn thesis were correct about the ghettoizing impact of multiculturalism, we would expect Canada to perform worse on these indicators of integration than other countries which have not adopted an official multiculturalism policy. Both Gwyn and Bissoondath contrast the Canadian approach with the American approach, which exclusively emphasizes common identities and common values, and refuses to provide public recognition or affirmation of ethnocultural differences. If Canada fared worse than the U.S. in terms of integrating immigrants, this would provide some indirect support for the Bissoondath/Gwyn theory.

In fact, however, Canada fares better than the United States on virtually any dimension of integration. Canada has higher naturalization rates than the United States—indeed, much higher, almost double. We also have higher rates of political participation, higher rates of official language acquisition, as well as lower rates of residential segregation. Canada also has much greater approval for intermarriage. Whereas 72% of Canadians approved of inter-racial marriages in 1988, only 40% of Americans approved of them, and 25% felt they should be illegal! And ethnicity is less salient as a determinant of friendship in Canada than the United States.

In short, on every indicator of integration, Canada, with its multiculturalism policy, fares better than the United States, with its repudiation of multiculturalism. We would find the same story if we compared Canada with other immigration countries which have rejected multiculturalism in favour of an exclusive emphasis on common identities—e.g., France.

Canada does better than these other countries, not only in our actual rates of integration, but also in our day-to-day sense of ethnic relations. In a 1997 survey, for example, people in twenty countries were asked whether they agreed that "different ethnic groups get along well here". The percentage of people who agreed was far higher in Canada (75%) than in the United States (58%) or France (51%).

This should not surprise us, since Canada does better than virtually any other country in the world in the integration of immigrants. The only comparable country is Australia, which is interesting, since it too has an official multiculturalism policy. Indeed, its multiculturalism policy was largely inspired by Canada's policy, although of course it has been adapted to Australia's circumstances.

The two countries which are head and shoulders above the rest of the world in the successful integration of immigrants are the two countries with official multiculturalism policies. They are much more successful than any country which has rejected multiculturalism.

In short, there is no evidence to support the claim that multiculturalism is promoting ethnic separateness or impeding immigrant integration. Whether we examine the trends within Canada since 1971, or compare Canada with other countries, the conclusion is the same—the multiculturalism program is working. It is achieving what it set out to do: helping to ensure that those people who wish to express their ethnic identity are respected and accommodated, while simultaneously increasing the ability of immigrants to integrate into the larger society. Along with our fellow multiculturalists in Australia, Canada does a better job of respecting ethnic diversity while promoting societal integration than any other country.

THE HISTORY OF NATIONS

Chapter 6

A Nation's Challenges

New Hopes for Native Peoples

By Andrew Purvis

In the following article, Time *magazine reporter Andrew Purvis examines the state of aboriginal communities in Canada at the close of the twentieth century. As he notes, the history of Canada's first nations in the five centuries since Europeans first began to settle North America has generally not been a happy one, and for the most part native communities in Canada today suffer from poverty, high unemployment, poor health care, and inadequate living conditions. According to Purvis, however, starting in the mid-1990s, the federal government has demonstrated renewed interest in addressing and resolving native issues. In addition to providing more money for native programs, federal and provincial governments are working to settle vast land claims and negotiate for native self-government. As Purvis points out, although many native people and nonnative Canadians welcome the impending changes, others are wary of their scope and consequences.*

When Minister of Indian Affairs Jane Stewart talks about the history of native peoples, it sounds as if Canada is in a recovery program. Violent standoffs of the early 1990s at Oka, Que., and other flash points are signs of "a dysfunctional relationship," she says. The Indian Act governing registered First Nations peoples is "parochial, paternalistic and controlling." The defunct residential-school system that took young native children off the reserve in the absence of their parents was a "tragedy." Stewart's warmth and volubility—not to mention her pop-psych jargon—seem out of place in the dark corridors of Parliament Hill. But there is no mistaking the conviction behind her words. The daughter of former Ontario Liberal leader Robert Nixon is determined to lead a revolution in native rights.

With little fanfare, Stewart's department has launched a reform program that aims to reverse more than a century of philosophy and practice in aboriginal affairs. Its consequences will be felt across the country—from the most remote Dene reserve in northern Alberta to the office towers of downtown Saskatoon, from the spruce forests of New Brunswick to the rolling farm-lands of southwestern Ontario. Other nations will be carefully weighing its success. The initiative goes by the name Gathering Strength, and its goal is to change forever the circumstances of the country's 800,000 aboriginal peoples—and those of many of the 29 million other Canadians who live with them.

A Bold Experiment

Most of the changes are under negotiation, and the full pattern is only beginning to emerge. But it includes a transfer of huge quantities of land and cash from both federal and provincial governments to native peoples for treaty rights that have eroded. Even more important, Ottawa [the capital of Canada, here used to refer to the federal government] intends to give native peoples extensive powers to guide their own destiny—a dramatic contrast to the fate of native peoples since before Confederation. It may be the boldest experiment in social justice in Canada's 140-year history. And as with all radical change, it has great potential for backlash.

Philosophically, Ottawa's initiative is bolder still. In effect, it hopes to bring a once-and-for-all end to the cultural destruction of aboriginal communities. In Ottawa's analysis, the ugly combination of joblessness, poverty, disease, ill health and delinquency that has strangled native peoples is caused above all by a lack of effective power. Supplying that elixir is the aim of reform. Says University of Toronto political scientist Peter Russell: "Indigenous peoples aren't going to have their own countries, but they are going to be consensual partners in the running of the country." Depending, of course, on what kind of consensus emerges.

In concrete terms, Prime Minister Jean Chretien's government intends to return to Canada's aboriginal peoples their due, from huge tracts of rock and ice in Labrador to the multimillion-dollar purchase price of new reserve land in Manitoba and Ontario to self-governing authority for every reserve or tribal council or Indian federation in the country. The two set-piece events that Canadians will witness this spring [1999]—ratification of the

Nisga'a agreement covering lands in British Columbia and the creation on April 1 of an autonomous Inuit-led government in the huge Arctic territory of Nunavut—are just the tip of reform. More negotiations are under way between Canada's aboriginal peoples and various levels of government than at any time in history. They include:

- About 80 different negotiations on self-government, most started up in the past two years. Some include Canada, the provinces and the First Nations. Others are bilateral. Talks range from one that deals only with who should operate on-reserve schools in Ontario to a Saskatchewan deal, near completion, in which Canada and the province will cede powers over the judiciary, policing, schools, child welfare and health care.
- Some 210 negotiations on land claims, ranging from so-called specific claims on treaty land (as small as one hectare [2.5 acres] or as large as 500,000 hectares [1.25 million acres]) to huge comprehensive land claims on territory where no treaties were ever inked. A deal may soon be settled in Labrador encompassing 15,800 sq km [6,100 square miles].
- An additional 280 preliminary land claims that are still being researched by the Department of Indian Affairs. This first stage can take up to five years. An average of 60 new claimants come forward each year, and 60% of those are accepted for negotiation.
- A handful of auxiliary talks or round tables that are springing up to support negotiations as they progress. These are focusing on subjects such as how to arrange future revenue and transfer payments between existing governments and a First Nations government and how to interpret the original "spirit and intent" of treaties signed more than a century ago. The purpose: to establish what issues or jurisdictions should be up for grabs.

It is all a confusing patchwork. Part of that is due to the First Nations' pursuing different agendas, part to variations in treaty history. Provinces also differ in their commitment to the whole initiative. Only British Columbia, Saskatchewan and Newfoundland recognize the inherent right to self-government of aboriginal peoples. And since the provinces hold key jurisdictions, such as lands and resources, they dictate what ends up on the table.

For all the helter-skelter nature of the process, one goal is clear. "The structure of the relationship between aboriginals and government has to change," Jane Stewart told TIME. "There will be battles, but in the end I am convinced that the result will be better than what we have today."

Mixed Opinions

Aboriginal leaders, for the most part, share her optimism, though some are still wary. Assembly of First Nations national chief Phil Fontaine heralds the push for "jurisdictional control" for Canada's Indians. "There's a clear recognition on the part of Ottawa that when we talk, it's not just First Nations to Indian Affairs. It's government to government."

Another big question is what most nonaboriginal Canadians think, and that is a mystery. In general, they have not been consulted. Negotiating sessions are closed to public view. But negotiators on all sides concede that better education, if not public relations, on the main points of Canada's legal and historic obligations would lessen the possibility of public uproar.

Experts who follow the process, however, are withholding judgment. University of Saskatchewan historian Jim Miller, author of a book on European-aboriginal relations in Canada, opines that "on balance, there are many more good things happening today than 10 years ago." But critics of federal policy, like University of Calgary political scientist Tom Flanagan, whose book *First Nations, Second Thoughts* is due out later this year [1999], argue that Ottawa is veering sharply down the wrong road. "We are heading into a period of intense conflict," warns the former Reform Party strategist.

The emphasis given by Ottawa to its native-rights initiative became apparent last summer [1998] during the signing ceremony for the controversial Nisga'a land deal. A horde of politicians, including Stewart and [British Columbia] Premier Glen Clark, descended on the remote town of New Aiyansh in northern British Columbia to witness the initialing of an accord that would affect about 5,500 people. Since then, Clark and Stewart have worked tirelessly to promote the deal and ensure its eventual ratification this spring in Victoria and Ottawa.

The Nisga'a deal is just one of many that are being negotiated on so-called untreatied land, where governments failed to sign any agreement in the past and where they are eager to tie up loose ends. Similar deals are being discussed throughout British Columbia and parts of northern Canada. Last month, British Columbia's Sechelt Indian band ended years of hard wrangling and legal grandstanding with an agreement in principle to settle their claim to nearly 1,000 hectares [2,500 acres] of prime urban and rural property along the spectacular Sunshine coast 50 km [30 miles] northwest of Vancouver. Provincial officials think that when all is settled, First Nations peoples will legally control 5% of British Columbia's area—in contrast to 0.3% for Indians nationwide.

Elsewhere in Canada, the emphasis is on redressing specific claims, in which land was surrendered in exchange for government assistance, but where First Nations say the government failed to live up to its end of the bargain. Last fall [1998] in Manitoba, 445,754 hectares [1.1 million acres] were handed back to 19 First Nations bands. Two months ago in southwestern Ontario, the 225-member Caldwell Indian band reached a tentative agreement worth $15.2 million to expand its reserve along the shores of Lake Erie. In Saskatchewan, 27 First Nations groups are spending more than $290 million awarded by Ottawa to purchase 635,363 hectares [1.6 million acres] of new reserve land.

Native Self-Government

Transfers of land and money are dramatic. But self-government talks may, in the end, prove more profound. At the moment they are nearly invisible. In Ontario, for instance, most of the talks are limited to bilateral discussions between bands and the federal government and mostly focus on a single jurisdiction, like education. One new southwestern Ontario deal transfers jurisdiction over primary and secondary education and on-reserve natural resources to eight First Nations known collectively as the United Anishnaabeg Councils. In the Atlantic provinces, two sets of such governance talks in Labrador involve huge swaths of territory, hundreds of millions of dollars and, in the case of the prospective Labrador Inuit Land, jurisdiction over the administration of schools, justice and social services.

By contrast, talks in British Columbia and Saskatchewan are often moving at a furious pace. Governments and sundry native groups are discussing ways to divvy up everything from child welfare and health jurisdiction to policing and even the judiciary. The Meadow Lake First Nation band on the Alberta-Saskatchewan border is scheduled to come to a far-reaching agreement in principle on March 31 [1999]. It calls for the transfer of powers governing band citizenship, lands and resources, education, health care and public works to the First Nation. Tax-levying powers and administration of justice are still being discussed.

Coupled with the specific talks is a broad-based effort to rediscover the original intent of treaties, in line with a 1997 Supreme Court of Canada decision, known as Delgamuukw, that gave native oral and tribal recollections of such deals equal status with the white man's paperwork. In Alberta, First Nations living on lands governed by Treaty 8, signed a century ago, have agreed to discussions with Ottawa on the original meaning of their treaty. In Saskatchewan, Indian elders gathered in five separate meetings 1 1/2 years ago [mid-1997] to record their version of the events surrounding treaty signings as passed down from their forefathers. The recorded testimony will be used in governance talks. "The question is how to interpret those treaties for the modern era," says David Hawkes, negotiator for Canada at the Saskatchewan talks. Federation of Saskatchewan Indian Nations (FSIN) chief Perry Bellegarde says these so-called treaty tables are fundamental. "Everything flows from them."

Ultimately, negotiators are looking to create three overlapping circles of government, with federal, provincial and First Nations authorities sharing some jurisdictions, such as health, and maintaining exclusive control over others, such as child welfare and education (for the First Nations) and national defense or currency (for Ottawa). Last December [1998] the Nova Scotia legislature passed the Micmac Education Act, which hands over legislative and administrative control of community schools to nine First Nations. In the Yukon, seven self-government deals have been struck. One of the first, signed by the Vuntut Gwitchin First Nation in 1993, provides a 25% share of royalties from future resources development on all traditional lands, as well as exclusive rights to all new big-game-outfitting concessions. Some deals include an Inuit agreement to give up exemption from provincial and federal sales tax.

Along with formal powers, native peoples are being given new weight as bureaucratic constituents. Ottawa and some provincial governments have begun to include native leadership in a wide range of official decision making. Organizations such as the Assembly of First Nations, Canada's largest aboriginal political grouping, are now regular participants even at the policy work-up stage in federal deliberations, says Minister Stewart. "The ways in which we can advance our causes are much smoother," says David Ahenakew, 65, national chief of the Assembly of First Nations from 1982 to 1985. "It's easier to get the little things done."

More Money for Native Programs

At least some of that goodwill is bought. Last year [1998], in the midst of buzz-saw cuts, the budget for Ottawa's Department of Indian Affairs climbed $390 million for new programs, plus a $228 million "healing fund" set up to address physical and psychological damage from Ottawa's residential school program. In

HEALING THE PAST

In the following excerpt from a 1998 speech delivered at Concordia University in Montreal, Phil Fontaine reflects on what European settlement meant for native people and shares his hopes for the future. At the time of the address, Fontaine was the national chief of the Assembly of First Nations.

I could spend the rest of my time here today describing the devastating poverty of our people, especially our young people, and its entrenchment in our communities. I could talk about race discrimination, suicide rates, high school drop out rates, police brutality, disproportionate diabetes and tuberculosis, ridiculously disproportionate imprisonment rates, past injustices, lies, double-dealing and the ongoing, unresolved grievances we continue to have with the government of Canada. I could describe these and other current problems, but I won't. Not today.

I won't because I have been asked to talk to you today about the next millennium. And if there is one thing I can promise you, it is that the *status quo* of First Nations today will not be the story of the next millennium. . . .

At this moment, more First Nation's citizens than ever before are participating in the development of our commu-

this month's [February 1999] federal budget, Stewart is asking for $375 million more than the department's current $3 billion slice for programs to spur economic development and boost education over the next four years. Stewart's budget is about the same as Industry Canada's and just under half the amount set aside for national defense.

Stewart's initiative has its roots in the confrontations that began the decade at Oka [the site of a long standoff between natives and Canada's armed forces, for control of ancestral burial grounds]. In their aftermath, the [Brian] Mulroney government appointed a seven-member Royal Commission on Aboriginal Peoples to study the problem. The commission's 3,500-page re-

---

nities—locally, regionally and nationally. We are looking critically at the social situations in which we find ourselves and we are taking the initiative to transform them to provide opportunities rather than take them away. Whether we are litigating in the Courts for recognition as partners in resource development decisions; negotiating treaties; participating in trade missions; or acquiring long overdue apologies and compensation for residential school abuse; we are taking it upon ourselves to change structures of society which until now have oppressed us. . . .

Although we are enthusiastically pursuing our vision, we cannot accomplish it alone. Investments must be made in Aboriginal economies, to restore individuals, families and communities to health, to create safe and healthy housing and useful community services, to provide appropriate education and to sustain our Aboriginal culture. If we can move along this path, we will enable our people to effectively occupy the roles required in the new relationship with the government and peoples of Canada. Our energy, converging with social and economic institutions and the Canadian government, can create a better future for all.

Phil Fontaine, "First Nations in Canada: A New Relationship for the Next Millennium," speech at Concordia University, Montreal, Quebec, October 27, 1998. Located at www.afn.ca.

port, released two years ago [1997], amply detailed the scope of the problems plaguing Canada's aboriginal peoples and argued for a comprehensive effort to relieve them. The solutions were sometimes derided for their cost, but Stewart, for one, was impressed: "If you read the report, you understand that people do want to be able to make decisions for themselves."

That view has got more than a little nudging from Canada's high courts in a series of increasingly bold decisions, culminating 14 months ago with the Delgamuukw decision, which affirmed for the first time that aboriginal title existed and laid out how it could be proved in a court of law. But such decisions are only symptoms of an even larger social shift. University of Toronto political scientist Russell, who has studied the growing political clout of indigenous peoples around the world, points to rising levels of aboriginal education and mastery of political tools as playing a major role in capturing government attention.

In Canada another factor is at work: the native population is booming. According to the 1996 census, the latest available figures, there are about 800,000 Indians, Inuit and Metis living in the country, 200,000 more than 30 years ago. The population will top 1 million by 2010. More than half the current population is under 25, and the overall rate of growth of aboriginal peoples is nearly twice that of the rest of the Canadian population. In Saskatchewan, by the year 2001, one-quarter of all people entering the work force and one-third of all new school entrants will be aboriginal.

Moreover, aboriginal populations are increasingly mainstream: about 42% of Canada's Indians live off the reserve, and that number has increased 50% over the past decade. Meantime, more than 85% of on-reserve households have incomes below the poverty line. Infant mortality is twice the national rate. Life expectancy is seven years below the norm, and suicide rates for women are four times that among other Canadian women.

A National Embarrassment

In December a report by the U.N. Committee on Economic, Social and Cultural Rights cited the "gross disparity" between the condition of aboriginal peoples and that of other Canadians. A comparison released by Indian Affairs noted that if Canada's on-reserve aboriginal population were viewed as a separate country in U.N. rankings that ordinarily trumpet Canada's accomplishments, it would fall somewhere below Mexico and Thailand and be on a par with Brazil. "It's an embarrassment," says federal negotiator and Carleton University professor David Hawkes. Minister Stewart agrees: "Canadians understand this difference, and they want it fixed."

There are some promising signs. Thirty years ago, 20 Indians were attending post-secondary institutions. Today the number is closer to 28,000. A generation of well-trained, well-educated leaders at ease with government is assuming power and helping tilt the economic scales a little. In Saskatchewan, for example, a gaming agreement signed two years ago between the FSIN and the provincial government created 1,000 jobs and is bringing in $13 million in revenues yearly.

Nonaboriginal Canadians so far appear of two minds about all these changes. Public-opinion polls show a consistent level of sympathy with the plight of First Nations peoples and a desire to provide some kind of relief for past wrongs. At the same time, there's a lot of anxiety about how far the changes should go, who will pay for them and whether anyone is keeping an eye on the till.

The University of Calgary's Flanagan, a vocal opponent of many recent Indian Affairs initiatives, believes the whole effort is ideologically bankrupt. "There is a doctrine of equivalence that holds that Indians were on the same level as Europeans when the settlers came," he says. "It's a theory originated by anthropologists and advanced by political activists." That belief, he argues, needs to be questioned before it becomes enshrined in public policy. Oral histories in particular—the new legal basis, after Delgamuukw, for claims of original title—need to be taken with a grain of salt.

Wary of Change

Flanagan's skepticism is echoed by others, especially in the West. The opposition Liberal Party in British Columbia has come down squarely against approval of the Nisga'a agreement unless the Clark government agrees to hold a province-wide referendum on the issue. "The people of British Columbia want to be sure that treaties reflect their values of equality," Liberal leader Gordon Campbell told TIME. The Nisga'a treaty, he says, "is taking away the rights of Canadians to vote for governments that will regulate their life." Elsewhere, the concept of self-government for the

First Nations is stirring considerable anxiety. "It scares the hell out of everyone," says David Miner, a Saskatchewan rancher who chairs a dispute-resolution committee to facilitate land purchases by local Indians. "It needs to be defined before you can begin to understand it." In the tiny farming community of Spiritwood, north of Saskatoon, longtime residents resisted attempts by the local Wichikan Lake band to purchase a swath of community pasture and turn it into a reserve after a major land-claims settlement. When the purchase was first proposed, it was voted down by an 88% majority. The offer was sweetened, and eventually the community came around grudgingly. "No sense in seeing it all go to hell," said rancher Grant Cadieu, 48, whose land borders the pasture. "But some people are still pretty sour about it."

Those sentiments may find deeper resonance in the months and years ahead. Less than a decade ago, 80% of Canadians told pollsters they supported the idea of native self-government. A poll commissioned last year [1998] by the Assembly of First Nations, by contrast, found that 50% of Canadians believed Indians can't properly manage their own affairs. In another sampling, the FSIN found that 45% of residents of the province had a "bad impression" of Indians, while 20% conceded only that they did not have a "boldly negative" assessment.

"Provincial governments go only as far as the polling will let them go," observes a veteran aboriginal politico from Saskatchewan. "The reason B.C. Liberal Party leader Campbell is expressing outrage is that there are a lot of people in B.C. who back him."

Many ordinary aboriginal people are equally wary of embracing self-government without safeguards to protect against the abuse of power. Some Indian leaders, like Saskatchewan's David Ahenakew, believe that all the governance tables should be scrapped in favor of one set of talks on how to split up the revenue from the land. "This whole haphazard approach is so incoherent," says Ahenakew, a former Canadian army sergeant who served in Korea and is now a senator with the FSIN. "You never know from year to year what kind of money you're going to get. You can't make plans." He says Stewart may have the best intentions, but something more radical is required.

What is no longer under discussion is the doctrine of assimilation, which most Indians have traditionally viewed as an affront and which Stewart's program officially consigns to the ash heap.

The new thinking, in its most optimistic form, embraces diversity as a national virtue. Yet real progress toward that goal will depend less on asserting cultural and political sovereignty than on seeking out common ground. As Stewart puts it, "It's not about difference; it's about finding a way for Indians and Inuit to really be a part of Canada." Like a vast tremor across the nation, forces are in motion to find that way; the shaking they will cause has just begun.

The Threat of Global Warming

By Alanna Mitchell

In the following article, Globe and Mail *journalist Alanna Mitchell reports on expert predictions that global warming will have an especially severe impact on Canada. According to Mitchell, Canada's reputation as "the great white north" won't protect it from the greenhouse effect, the name given to a rise in average temperature caused by high levels of carbon dioxide in the atmosphere. Already, she says, Inuit in northern Canada have observed the thinning of polar ice-fields and fewer polar bears than usual. Experts warn that, in time, global warming may well destroy nearly one-half of Canada's life-sustaining habitats, causing great harm to its animal and human population.*

Fast-forward 100 years and here's the Canada you can expect to see: Pacific waters too warm to support salmon. An Arctic too balmy for the handful of skinny polar bears left on the Earth. Massive forests so short of water that they crack and fall.

In fact, according to a groundbreaking study published yesterday [August 30, 2000] in Toronto by the World Wide Fund for Nature (formerly World Wildlife Fund), Canada is expected to be among the countries worst hit by human-caused global warming.

The study predicts that roughly 46 per cent of the life-sustaining habitats that exist in Canada will be destroyed if the levels of carbon dioxide now being sent into the atmosphere are not cut down.

Other habitats may replace those that disappear, but they could be wastelands devoid of life. Scientists are worried that such icons of Canadian nature as freshwater trout, ducks and caribou will not be nimble enough to survive in healthy numbers.

"Do we as humans have to have a future where we destroy everything?" asked Dr. Jay Malcolm, an ecologist in the faculty of forestry at the University of Toronto and an author of the study. "I think we as a species can do better than that."

The report, Global Warming and Terrestrial Biodiversity Decline, uses computer models to show how climate and plant life are expected to change as greenhouse gases increase in the atmosphere, trapping heat above the Earth.

Then it poses questions not asked before. How much habitat will be lost the world over? How fast will plants and animals have to migrate in order to get to new systems that can support them? How many species will become extinct in this human-caused catastrophe?

Impending Catastrophe

The answer is what Dr. Malcolm calls the weeds-of-the-world-unite scenario. Weed species—think rats or crab grass or cockroaches—stand to do quite well. Other forms of life that don't adapt quite as quickly, or that are fragile anyway because so much of their habitat is already gone, could disappear forever.

"This has the potential to cause sweeping ecological change and significant species loss. And it's a particularly bleak situation for Canada," Dr. Malcolm said.

The study deliberately uses conservative predictions, he said. They rely on the premise that the amount of carbon dioxide in the atmosphere will double from preindustrial levels by the end of this century. Other reputable computer programs forecast a tripling of the levels during that period, a scenario that would result in far more dramatic change on the ground.

David Suzuki, the Canadian geneticist and broadcaster who has set up an environmental foundation in his name, said yesterday at the launch of the new study that these scenarios are all the more troubling because solutions exist to forestall them. He rhymed off a spate of international promises Canada has made, pledging to reduce the greenhouse gases emitted over Canadian lands.

The latest, the Kyoto agreement of 1997 that pledged to bring Canadian emissions of carbon dioxide to the level of 6 per cent below those of 1990 by the year 2010, is unlikely to be met.

"What does it take to get any type of action from our political leaders?" Dr. Suzuki asked.

He added that the Kyoto protocols, which have attracted heavy fire from the auto and petroleum industries in Canada, are merely a first step in what must be a long-term plan to keep the

Earth's temperature from rising as far and as fast as the computer models predict. Other types of greenhouse gases, notably the dreaded methane, which is far more heat-trapping than carbon dioxide, will also have to be controlled, he said.

The Threat to Canadians

That temperature rise is expected to range from 2 C to 8 C on average in Canada during the next 100 years, if not sooner. To put that in perspective, consider that during the Ice Age 13,000 years ago, when Canada was covered in glaciers, the average temperature here was about five degrees colder than it is today. Then, the woolly mammoth and the sabre-tooth tiger ruled. The tundra was at Pennsylvania.

When the ice retreated and the temperature rose, creating new habitats, plants and animals moved in. If nothing changes, greenhouse-gas emissions will warm up the Earth about 10 times faster than during the natural passing of the Ice Age. Dr. Malcolm believes this rate of warming is unprecedented.

Humans are already feeling the effects of global warming. In the Arctic, where warming is more pronounced than in other parts of the world, the Inuit see thinning ice and fewer polar bears, said Violet Ford, an environmental-policy adviser to the Inuit Tapirisat of Canada. Those changes and others mean that the Inuit have more trouble living off the land, she said.

Humans in more southerly regions will face changes, too, unless greenhouse gases retreat, said Monte Hummel, president of the Canadian arm of the World Wide Fund for Nature, the Switzerland-based conservation organization best known for its international campaign to save the panda.

He predicted more respiratory problems, wide-scale losses in jobs in the resource industries and higher taxes as governments are called on to help humans adapt to new climates.

"These will not be abstract experiences," he said.

Free Trade Threatens Canada's Independence

By Peter C. Newman

In the following selection, Peter C. Newman, one of Canada's most re-
spected journalists and nonfiction writers, discusses free trade and its effect
on Canada. According to Newman, the Free Trade Area of the Americas,
a proposed free trade domain covering virtually all of North and South
America, would mean the end of Canada as an independent economic
and political unit. Newman argues that the proposed trade agreement
would inevitably deepen U.S. domination of the hemisphere, given the
economic size of the United States. As Newman sees it, unless the trend
toward freer trade is checked, Canada will lose its own currency and ulti-
mately enter into a political union with the United States, a prospect he
finds unappealing.

Free trade, the issue that dominated Canadian politics during the past two decades, was remarkably absent in the recent election campaign [Fall 2000]. . . .

At the dawn of a new year, we are faced with historic trade
initiatives that may detonate an economic revolution significantly
affecting the three national entities that share this continent—
none more profoundly than Canada. (The Americans possess so
much disposable clout that their autonomy is assured; the Mexicans have the advantage of a distinctive culture.)

The unusual confluence of the continent's trio of newly
elected political leaders assuming power within a few months of
each other may be an accident of history. But their agendas, hidden and otherwise, threaten this country's future in dramatic

Peter C. Newman, "End of Canada? Measures to Expand Free Trade Will
Inevitably Lead to the End of First Our Dollar—and Then Our Sovereignty,"
Maclean's, vol. 114, January 8, 2001, pp. 18–20. Copyright © 2001 by Maclean's
Magazine. Reproduced by permission.

ways, and are bound to turn the trade issue into one of the major political debates of 2001.

The controversy will be fuelled by an unprecedented meeting
of 34 Western Hemisphere leaders, to be held in Quebec City
in late April [2001], to draft a treaty for a Free Trade Area of the
Americas. Because any trading arrangement in this global quad-
rant is bound to be dominated by the United States, such an
agreement would in reality become the modern version of the
Monroe Doctrine of 1823. Named after U.S. president James
Monroe, it was a bald attempt to define the Americas as an exclusive sphere of U.S. influence. That imperialist impulse was
aimed at giving Washington economic and political sway over
anything that moved between Alert at the frozen edge of
Ellesmere Island in the Canadian Arctic, to Cape Horn, the
wind-swept tip of South America. This treaty, despite its multi-
national roots, will have a similar effect.

Expanding Trade Agreements

Few of the proponents or opponents of the hotly contested, but
relatively innocent, 1989 Free Trade Agreement, signed between
prime minister Brian Mulroney and president Ronald Reagan,
realized that this was the beginning, not the end, of a long
process. Historically, such pacts almost always evolve in directions
far removed from their original intent.

Countries that agree to lower mutual tariffs, which is what the
Canada–U.S. Free Trade Agreement was essentially about, inevitably become caught up in an escalation of these primitive
arrangements. This inexorable process begins with a Free Trade
Area becoming a Customs Union, which significantly widens its
scope to include goods from third world countries. We started
down that path when Mulroney signed the North American Free
Trade Agreement (NAFTA) with then-President George Bush
(the older, smarter one) and the then-president of Mexico, Car-
los Salinas. The momentum currently building up would escalate
NAFTA, which went into effect on Jan. 1, 1994, into a Common
Market. That's a Customs Union that integrates the economies of
its partners to include the free movement of labour and capital.

Ever since Vicente Fox Quesada won the Mexican election
last summer [2000], he has been advocating such a pact, and neither Washington nor Ottawa has rejected his advances. As the example of the European Common Market illustrates, this arrange-

ment has within it the built-in impetus to turn into an Economic Union. That's a Common Market, plus a pledge by member states to correlate and eventually merge all of their economic (and not just trade) policies. Out of those initiatives, Europe is now rapidly advancing towards Economic Integration, which is an Economic Union, plus the unification of not just monetary and fiscal policies, but social measures as well.

The Loss of Independence

Few are advocating a similar arrangement on this side of the Atlantic. Yet. But even the move to a Common Market, which implies an eventual common North American currency, would mean nothing less than the disappearance of Canada as an effective, independent nation. A North American Common Market would mean the free movement of people and money throughout the continent. The Canadian dollar would disappear as part of this process, which would mean that we could never again control either our fiscal or monetary policies. We would, in effect, become the northern district of Washington's Federal Reserve Board. Canadians would be free to leave and find work anywhere in the United States, as would Mexicans who wish to move to Canada, where they would compete for many of our blue-collar jobs at half the going rate. Such a deal would place this country in the jaws of a magnet that would reorient whatever is left of our founding east west linkages and reroute our railways, highways, truck routes, telecommunications systems, as well as requiring the building of "non-energy pipelines," which sound suspiciously like carriers of Canadian water to U.S. destinations.

Economic Dependence

Even now, Canada's economic dependence on the United States is overwhelming. Some 87 per cent of our exports—goods worth nearly $1 billion—flow daily across the 49th parallel. At the same time, our industries are becoming U.S.-owned at an alarming rate, while a quarter of the leading Canadian companies on the Toronto Stock Exchange currently report their earnings in U.S. dollars.

Already, powerful American think-tanks, such as the Carnegie Endowment for International Peace, are recommending the disappearance of the Canada-U.S. border. "It is our contention," concludes their July [2000] study Self Governance at the Border, "that, substantively at least, the U.S.-Canada border is likely to dis-appear before any politician finds the courage to negotiate its re-moval." Mulroney, the author of the original Free Trade Agree-ment, has openly advocated the borderless option. "I would certainly support getting rid of all this stuff at the borders, which inhibits progress and the free movement of goods, services and people," he declared in an interview last year. Most significant, the Business Council on National Issues, which gets what it wants, has supported the notion of a seamless border that would allow the free movement of goods and services in both directions.

In this context, it was no accident that Jean Chretien chose to give his first speech as the country's newly crowned Prime Min-ister by unexpectedly appearing at the World Summit on the Arts and Culture, meeting in Ottawa, four days after the election. In-stead of stressing the obvious point that in a global economy, it's only the vigour of any nation's indigenous culture that can guar-antee its independence, he emphasized exactly the opposite no-tion. "Some people," he told the delegates, "think that the Amer-ican culture is a problem. It's not a problem. . . . Don't be afraid to be citizens of the world."

That declaration was particularly surprising, since Chretien is well aware how tough it is to wring any concessions from the Americans. He won his first majority in the 1993 election, partly by pledging to rewrite NAFTA, negotiated under the Mulroney government, so that its provisions would be tilted more in Canada's favour. One of his main attacks was on a restrictive pro-vision that allowed the Americans to retaliate against Canada if we adopted any measures to strengthen our culture. That key de-mand and Chretien's other substantive requests were rejected out of hand by the Americans.

The specifics of the debate over Canada joining a North American Common Market have yet to be set. At the moment, no one knows who will speak for Canada. Certainly, the Chre-tien government has been making loud continentalist noises, and the Alliance's [the Canadian Alliance, a political party] convic-tion that market forces should control national destinies disqual-ifies them as Canadian nationalism's champions. In truth, there are few independent voices manning the barricades, and Mitchell Sharp last May celebrated his 89th birthday.

Ironically, Sharp, former external affairs minister in the Trudeau government, now a senior adviser to Chretien, is one of the very few Canadian politicians who ever issued a public warning about the long-term impact of free trade. "Free trade," he wrote in a 1972 policy paper, long before such a radical idea was contemplated by any Canadian political party, "tends towards a full customs union and economic union as a matter of internal logic. A Canada-U.S. free trade area would almost certainly do likewise. If this were to happen, Canada would be obliged to seek political union with its superpower neighbour."

That certainly was an opinion shared by one of the most powerful American public figures of the time, George Ball, a former undersecretary of state, and much-listened-to animator among Washington's continentalist advocates. Predicting the future course of American-Canadian relations, he wrote in his 1968 book, *The Discipline of Power:* "Sooner or later, commercial imperatives will bring about free movement of all goods back and forth across our long border; and when that occurs, or even before it does, it will become unmistakably clear that countries with economies so inextricably intertwined must also have free movement of the other vital factors of production—capital, services and labour. The result will inevitably be substantial economic integration, which will require for its full realization a progressively expanding area of common political decision."

Those long-ago echoes will shape the debate that will unexpectedly dominate Canadian politics in the months and years ahead. While the topic of the debate will be a new North American trading arrangement, its substance will be the fate of our economy, the destiny of our natural resources and the opportunities for our children. Nothing short of Canada's independence will be at stake.

[Editor's note: As of October 2002, negotiations regarding the Free Trade Area of the Americas are still ongoing.]

U.S.-Canadian Relations in the Aftermath of September 11

By Desmond Morton

In the following address, Desmond Morton, a Canadian historian, argues that the terrorist attacks of September 11, 2001, will lead to closer ties between Canada and the United States. According to Morton, Canada recognized in the early years of the Second World War that its national security could be best preserved in an alliance with the United States. Similarly, he argues, in the aftermath of September 11, Canada must either integrate its security with that of the United States or risk huge trade losses as border shipments are delayed or curtailed because of security concerns. Morton notes that some Canadians believe closer ties with the United States will undermine Canadian sovereignty, but he argues that Canada's distinct national policies on immigration, social services, and culture can survive closer union with the United States.

September 11 will have a place in 21st century history, though how precisely it will appear, no sensible historian should predict. The event opens an "asymmetric" war, a kind of global jiu-jitsu, in which the wealth and resources of a super-power are used for its own destruction. It is a conflict without limits or point.

But who are the enemy? Was the September 11 attack the first of a new series of horrors or simply another cycle in an endless series? Unlike economists and politicians, historians should wait until at least most of the facts are known. Routinely I warn students to mistrust me on any event since 1930. The Chinese, we

Desmond Morton, "Asymmetric War Ties Canada Closer to U.S.," *Canadian Speeches*, vol. 15, September/October 2001, pp. 10–12. Copyright © 2001 by Desmond Morton. Reproduced by permission.

are told, are still waiting to see what the French Revolution really meant. What is caution when acres of newsprint must be inked and endless hours of television filled with surmise, rumour, and paranoia? I did my bit, joining those who may have encouraged potential terrorists of all varieties to achieve their own moment of gory glory. Wrap-around publicity on CNN, ABC and even the CBC [Canadian Broadcasting Corporation] became an even more certain reward than an Islamic paradise.

A War at Home

Since 9 A.M. on September 11, media savants have assured us that things will never be the same again. The same is true of September 10 and 12. Any day, however drab, adds a tiny accretion to the past. September 11 was different, less as a date of massive terrorism, but because the violence invaded what the American military used to call the ZI—the Zone of the Interior. Not since our side burned the White House in the War of 1812 had Americans experienced a foreign-planned attack on their own soil. Pearl Harbor was outside the ZI, in the mid-Pacific. On September 11, Americans woke up feeling utterly secure: by 0930, they felt utterly vulnerable, uncertain even of whence the attack had come.

Details are slowly becoming clear. Consequences will follow. For Canada, they will be direct and substantial. In mid-1940, Canadians stood in terrible peril, the second largest member of the frail alliance that stood up to Hitler's Germany. That August, Canada integrated its security with the only country that had ever tried to conquer us. The Ogdensburg agreement was logical, beneficial, and a little painful for those nostalgic for Britain's power. But hadn't the British themselves concluded 80 years before that they could not defend us? Our political leaders had the good sense to agree, and the Ogdensburg agreement was a long-deferred but logical next step. No one in Ottawa foresaw all the consequence but in 1944 a wise general, Maurice Pope, warned that Washington would require us to maintain a higher standard of national security than most Canadians could probably justify. A fresh payment is due.

If American isolationism had resumed after 1945, Canada might have escaped some of the costs and dangers of the Cold War. Like most Americans, we learned our lesson. Instead, Ottawa mandarins did their utmost to involve the United States in the United Nations and world problems. In 1949, NATO became our "provincial solution," not merely to unite our European homeland against Stalin's armies but also to engage the Americans in the same task—while acquiring allies to help moderate Washington's unpredictable enthusiasm. Meanwhile, in those postwar years, Canadians built an unprecedented prosperity in an increasingly bilateral partnership with the world's richest country. We had left an enfeebled ally in 1940 to join another with vastly larger resources. Alliances cost less than independence but there was and is a fee.

North American defence has been an amazing success story. One hundred and ninety-two years of immunity from foreign attack must be a world record. Now Americans want their peace of mind restored and its disruption avenged. Canadians—still enjoying their fragile immunity—must expect to help restore American peace of mind. At stake is our economic partnership. Canadian nationalists, dismayed at our Faustian bargain, may claim that trade has nothing to do with security. They should visit the border and they should talk to their next-door neighbours. In the wake of September 11, Canadians felt as united with Americans as they were with Britain in either world war. The most audible complaints were that [Prime Minister] Jean Chretien had neglected the cry of "Ready, Aye Ready" that Sir Wilfrid Laurier [then prime minister] had offered Britain in 1914.

Most Canadians were still British in 1914; they now identify with Americans. They, or their children, dreamt of working in the World Trade Center, and some of them did. We, too, felt violated.

Emotions will subside. The intellectuals who hurried to lay the blame on the Americans will rally supporters. But the realities of a trade-dependent country with only one substantial customer will persist. We either defend the gates of America or we shall sit outside. Ottawa recognized reality in the NORAD [North American Aerospace Defense Command] agreement of 1957 and we have renewed it faithfully, even in years when its specific threat had faded. If the United States sets up its Homeland Defence without Canada, both countries will be less secure and Canadians will find themselves very much poorer.

This is not simply because Canada has neglected its security while Americans need only a few costly but quick fixes. Each neighbour imitates the other's strengths and weaknesses. Both have vibrant traditions of civil liberty. Both defend ideological pluralism and have trouble distinguishing "freedom fighters" from terrorists. Both countries cherish due process, and independent judiciary, the benefit of the doubt. Both suspect bureaucracy and both should. Both countries have a variety of security services with no love of sharing secrets. We have CSIS [Canadian Security Intelligence Service], the RCMP [Royal Canadian Mounted Police]; they have the CIA, the FBI, and we both have a welter of local police forces. Both countries dumped responsibility for airport security on airlines, knowing they were on the verge of bankruptcy. We are both multicultural societies with large immigrant populations. The vast majority of newcomers pocket their pride, learn new ways, and prosper; a few are as prone to anger, resentment and pathological behaviours as native-born citizens, and they find overseas allies more easily.

Both countries will need all the genius they can muster to make security systems work without destroying the rights and freedoms which far outrank material affluence as our principal contributions to human civilization. Will this cost Canada its sovereignty? Only if Canadians insist on it, and polls suggest that, overwhelmingly, we won't. Distinct national policies on immigration, social services, culture, defence, and most other traditional sovereign powers have survived a European Union and a common frontier for people and goods. We can do so too—if we want.

CHRONOLOGY

18,000–10,000 B.C.
The first people migrate to North America.

A.D. 700–1000
The Inuit migrate to North America.

1004–1005
Leif Eriksson spends the winter in Vinland, now L'Anse aux Meadows, Newfoundland.

1497
John Cabot reaches Cape Breton Island and claims the land for England's King Henry VII.

1534
On July 7 the first-known meeting of Europeans and native peoples occurs when Jacques Cartier trades furs with the Micmac; later that month he lands at the entrance to the St. Lawrence River and claims the land for France's King Francis I.

1603
Samuel de Champlain reaches Canada.

1608
Champlain founds Quebec.

1625
Jesuits arrive in New France to bring Christianity to native peoples.

1639
The Algonquin and Huron nations suffer substantial losses from smallpox, which arrives with Europeans.

1642
Montreal is founded.

1670
The Hudson's Bay Company is chartered.

1735
The French complete the fortress Louisbourg on Ile-Royale, Cape Breton, then the strongest fort on the continent.

1749
Halifax is founded on the eastern shores of Nova Scotia.

1756
The Seven Years' War begins when Britain declares war on France; it is a war for Canada and to determine the boundaries of the thirteen colonies.

1758
Quebec City falls to the British after the battle of the Plains of Abraham.

1763
Under the Treaty of Paris, signed by the British, French, and Spanish, Britain acquires sovereignty over most of North America.

1774
The British Parliament passes the Quebec Act, which grants certain rights to the French in British North America.

1770s–1780s
United Empire Loyalists arrive by the thousands, fleeing persecution in the newly established United States.

1783
Article 1 of the Treaty of Versailles recognizes the United States and establishes its first northern border.

1784
Loyalists establish the province of New Brunswick.

1791
The Constitution Act creates Upper and Lower Canada.

1793
Alexander Mackenzie is the first person known to cross the continent north of Mexico, reaching the Pacific Ocean.

1812

U.S. president James Madison declares war on Britain, which includes Canada.

1814

The war ends with the Treaty of Ghent.

1818

The forty-ninth parallel is established as the northern U.S. border by the Convention of 1818.

1829

The last-known member of the Beothuk people dies in Newfoundland.

1837

Rebellions break out and are put down in Upper and Lower Canada.

1839

Lord Durham issues his report on the affairs of British North America.

1840

The British Parliament creates the province of Canada, a merger of Upper and Lower Canada.

1845

John Franklin sets out, for the third time, to find the Northwest Passage; he never returns.

1851

A census indicates that, for the first time, anglophones outnumber francophones.

1854

The United Province of Canada and the United States sign their first reciprocity treaty.

1867

The British North America Act is passed by the British Parliament; it unites the Province of Canada with New Brunswick and Nova Scotia into the self-governing Dominion of Canada; Sir John A. Macdonald is Canada's first prime minister.

1870
Manitoba enters confederation.

1871
British Columbia enters confederation.

1872
In April the Dominion Lands Act lets the federal government retain control of all public lands in western Canada; in June the federal government's Trade Unions Bill lets workers join unions.

1873
Prince Edward Island enters confederation.

1876
The Indian Act is passed, putting natives in the legal category of wards of the state.

1880
Britain passes control of Arctic islands to Canada.

1884
Laws are passed prohibiting certain aboriginal cultural practices, and the responsibility for education of first nation children is given in large part to Christian residential schools.

1885
The Canadian Pacific Railway is completed; Louis Riel, who led a Métis revolt in Manitoba, is hanged.

1893
The Montreal Amateur Athletic Association wins the first Stanley Cup in hockey.

1896
In July Wilfrid Laurier becomes the first francophone prime minister; in November the government initiates the biggest immigration drive in the nation's history, seeking to settle the prairie provinces by attracting immigrants with farming experience.

1903
The boundary between Canada and Alaska is established.

1905

Alberta and Saskatchewan join the confederation; the Naval Services Act creates the Canadian navy.

1914

Canada is automatically at war when Britain declares war on
Germany.

1917

In August the Military Services Act establishes conscription,
which Quebec deeply resents; in December a French munitions ship explodes near Halifax, destroying much of the city
and killing over one thousand people.

1918

In April riots break out in Quebec in opposition to conscription;
in May women win the right to vote in federal elections; in
November World War I ends.

1919

A general strike in Winnipeg lasts over a month.

1920

The Royal Canadian Mounted Police is founded.

1926

The Imperial Conference adopts the Balfour Report, which recognizes Canada as an autonomous entity within the British
Empire.

1927

The Indian Act is amended to make it illegal for first nations to
raise money or hire a lawyer to advance land claims.

1930

Cairine Wilson becomes the first woman in the Canadian
Senate.

1931

The British Parliament passes the Statute of Westminster, which
grants British dominions, including Canada, legal freedom.

1936

The Canadian Broadcasting Corporation is founded.

1939

In May the National Film Board is founded; in September Canada, independently of Britain, declares war on Germany.

1940

Quebec recognizes women's right to vote in provincial elections, the last province to do so.

1944

Canadian prime minister William Lyon Mackenzie King hosts British prime minister Winston Churchill and U.S. president Franklin Roosevelt at Quebec to discuss the future of the war.

1945

Canada, along with forty-nine other nations, signs the World Security Charter, creating the United Nations.

1946

The Canadian Citizenship Act is passed; until this act, Canadians were recognized as Britons by other countries.

1949

In March Newfoundland and Labrador enter confederation; in April the North Atlantic Treaty Organization, the establishment of which was proposed by Prime Minister Louis St. Laurent, unites Canada, the United States, and ten European countries for mutual defense; in December Canada acquires the power to amend the British North America Act.

1950

Canadian units enter the Korean War.

1951

Parliament repeals the Indian Act ban on cultural activities and land claims and begins to dismantle the residential school system.

1952

Vincent Massey becomes the first governor general born in Canada.

1954

The Toronto subway, Canada's first, opens.

1955

Canada and the United States agree that the United States will build a distant early warning radar network in northern Canada and Alaska.

1956

The Female Employees Equal Pay Act guarantees equal pay to men and women doing the same, or substantially the same, work.

1957

In June, Ellen Fairclough becomes the first female cabinet minister; in September Canada and the United States form NORAD, the North American Air Defense Command; in October Lester B. Pearson wins the Nobel Peace Prize for his Suez Canal peace plan.

1960

In March Parliament grants native peoples federal franchise; in August the Bill of Rights becomes law.

1962

The Trans-Canada Highway is completed.

1964

Canada adopts a new flag, the now-familiar red maple leaf on a white background between two red bars.

1965

The Royal Commission calls for universal health care, with minimum standards across the country.

1966

The Medical Care Act provides universal health care.

1967

French president Charles de Gaulle visits Montreal and shouts to a crowd, *"Vive le Quebec libre!"* ("Long live free Quebec!"), causing a controversy.

1968

René Lévesque founds the Parti Québécois, which pushes for a sovereign Quebec.

1969
The Official Languages Act makes both English and French the official languages of Canada.

1970
Prime Minister Pierre Trudeau invokes the War Measures Act in response to terrorist activities by Quebec separatists.

1972
Canadian pride swells when the Canadian men's hockey team defeats the Soviet Union late in the eighth game to win the Canada–Soviet Union Summit Series.

1976
In July capital punishment is abolished for all civilian crimes; in November the separatist Parti Québécois wins the Quebec provincial election and promises to hold a referendum on sovereignty.

1977
Quebec's parliament passes Bill 101, which requires all children to attend French school unless one of the child's parents attended an English grade school.

1980
In February Jeanne Sauvé becomes the first female speaker of the House of Commons; in May Quebecers vote 59 percent to 41 percent against separation; in June "O Canada" is adopted as the national anthem.

1981
Quebec bans public signs in English.

1982
Queen Elizabeth II signs a royal proclamation patriating the constitution, which amends the British North America Act and includes the Charter of Rights and Freedoms; neither Quebec nor the first nations were in favor of the patriation.

1983
Jeanne Sauvé becomes the first female governor general.

1984

The Canada Health Act, which lets the federal government with-
hold funding of provincial health programs if they fail to be
public and nonprofit, comprehensive, universal, portable, and
accessible, is passed unanimously by the House of Commons.

1988

In January Prime Minister Brian Mulroney and U.S. president
Ronald Reagan sign the North American Free Trade Agreement; in December the Supreme Court strikes down the
Quebec law specifying that public commercial signs can be
in French only; later that month the premier of Quebec uses
section 33 of the Canadian Charter of Rights and Freedoms
to enforce the sign law.

1990

In June the Meech Lake Constitutional Accord, a plan to address
Quebec's constitutional concerns, fails to be approved by the
Manitoba and Newfoundland legislatures; in July Lucien
Bouchard, formerly a liberal cabinet minister, founds the Bloc
Québécois, the goal of which is to push for an autonomous
Quebec.

1991

In June the Quebec government signs an agreement with the
Barriere Lake Algonquin band, giving them some control
over their ancestral lands, in a deal that is the first of its kind;
in August, Ontario becomes the first province to recognize
native rights to self-government; in December the federal
government and the Inuit agree to create a huge new territory in the north known as Nunavut.

1992

In April the United Nations ranks Canada as the world's best
country in which to live, an honor it will hold for the next
eight years; in October voters in a national referendum reject
the Charlottetown Accord, which had proposed recognition
of aboriginal rights to self-government and stronger rights
for Quebec; in December the leaders of Canada, the United
States, and Mexico formally sign the North American Free
Trade Agreement.

1993

In June, Kim Campbell, who replaced Brian Mulroney as leader
of the Progressive Conservative Party, becomes the first female prime minister; in August the federal government shuts
down the east coast cod fishing industry due to overfishing.

1994

The Parti Québécois wins the Quebec provincial election; its
goal is the separation of Quebec from Canada.

1995

Quebec voters decide by a thin margin (50.6 percent to 49.4 percent) not to separate from Canada; earlier, the Cree first nation and the Inuit in northern Quebec voted 95 percent in
favor of staying in Canada if Quebecers voted for sovereignty.

2000

The Nisga'a Final Agreement is passed by the Senate, having
been ratified in the House of Commons, the British Columbia provincial legislature, and by the Nisga'a first nation;
the deal, the first modern land-claims treaty in British Columbia, includes 1,992 square kilometers of land, hunting
and fishing rights, $190 million over fifteen years, and funds
for transition and other projects; it also provides the Nisga'a
with self-government.

For Further Research

Books

Pierre Berton, *My Country: The Remarkable Past*. Toronto: McClelland and Stewart, 1976.

Robert Craig Brown, *The Illustrated History of Canada*. Toronto: Lester, 1991.

Robert Craig Brown and Ramsay Cook, *Canada, 1896–1921: A Nation Transformed*. Toronto: McClelland and Stewart, 1974.

Jean R. Burnett, ed., *Coming Canadians: An Introduction to a History of Canada's Peoples*. Toronto: McClelland and Stewart, 1988.

William D. Coleman, *The Independence Movement in Quebec, 1945–1980*. Toronto: University of Toronto Press, 1984.

Ramsay Cook, *French Canadian Nationalism: An Anthology*. Toronto: MacMillan of Canada, 1969.

Donald Creighton, *The Forked Road: Canada, 1939–1954*. Toronto: McClelland and Stewart, 1976.

———, *The Road to Confederation: The Emergence of Canada, 1863–1867*. Toronto: MacMillan of Canada, 1964.

Olive Patricia Dickason, *Canada's First Nations: A History of Founding Peoples from the Earliest Times*. Toronto: McClelland and Stewart, 1992.

John A. Dickinson and Brian Young, *A Short History of Quebec*. Toronto: Copp Clark Pitman, 1993.

Barry Gough, *Canada*. Englewood Cliffs, NJ: Prentice-Hall, 1975.

Victor Howard, *Creating the Peaceable Kingdom and Other Essays on Canada*. East Lansing: Michigan State University Press, 1998.

Desmond Morton, *A Short History of Canada.* Toronto: McClelland and Stewart, 1995.

Gerard Pelletier, *The October Crisis.* Toronto: McClelland and Stewart, 1971.

Mordecai Richler, *Oh Canada! Oh Quebec! Requiem for a Divided Country.* Toronto: Penguin, 1992.

John Herd Thompson and Stephen J. Randall, *Canada and the United States: Ambivalent Allies.* Athens: University of Georgia Press, 1997.

Susan Mann Trofimenkoff and Alison Prentice, eds., *The Neglected Majority: Essays in Canadian Women's History.* Toronto: Copp Clark Pitman, 1986.

Robin Winks, *The Blacks in Canada.* Montreal: McGill-Queen's University Press, 1997.

Periodicals

David S. Broder, "Canada's Unity: The Issue Behind the Vote," *Washington Post*, May 20, 1979.

DeNeed L. Brown, "Culture Corrosion in Canada's North; Forced into the Modern World, Indigenous Inuit Struggle to Cope," *Washington Post*, July 16, 2001.

———, "High on Gas and Low on Hope; In Canada's Northeast, Innu Children Take Up Deadly Addiction," *Washington Post*, December 21, 2000.

John F. Burns, "Canadian Church Approves Homosexual Ministers," *New York Times*, August 28, 1988.

William Claiborne, "Indians Gather as Siege Intensifies; Armed Confrontation in Canada Reflects Growing Militancy," *Washington Post*, July 19, 1990.

———, "Quebec Sovereignty: What Would Become of Canada?" *Washington Post*, December 28, 1990.

Ian Darragh, "Quebec's Quandary," *National Geographic*, November 1997.

Robertson Davies, "Signing Away Canada's Soul," *Harper's*, January 1989.

Herbert H. Denton, "Canada: A Unique Hybrid System," *Washington Post*, July 7, 1987.

——, "Canada Moves on Native Land Rights; Agreement Would Give Northwest Territories More Local Control," *Washington Post*, September 7, 1988.

Dusko Doker, "Quebec Voters Defeat Proposal for Independence from Canada; Quebec Autonomy Proposal Defeated," *Washington Post*, May 20, 1980.

Economist, "Bleeding-Heart Conservatives," October 8, 1988.

David R. Francis, "Why Canada Is Safer than US," *Christian Science Monitor*, January 2, 1987.

Henry Giniger, "Separatism Grows in Western Canada," *New York Times*, November 30, 1980.

Michael Kaufman, "Canada: An American Discovers Its Difference," *New York Times Magazine*, May 15, 1983.

Guy Lawson, "No Canada?" *Harper's*, April 1996.

Paul Lewis, "Canada About to Sign Major Land Agreement with Eskimos," *New York Times*, August 21, 1989.

Constance Matthiessen, "Should the U.S. Copy Canada?" *Washington Post*, November 27, 1990.

Karl Meyer, "O (Backward) Canada," *New York Times*, December 26, 1980.

Steven Pearlstein, "O Canada! A National Swan Song? U.S. Economic, Cultural Weight Threaten Nation's Identity," *Washington Post*, September 5, 2000.

Mordecai Richler, "Letter from Ottawa: The Sorry State of Canadian Nationalism," *Harper's*, June 1975.

Howard Schneider, "Canada: A Mosaic, Not a Melting Pot; Fast-Growing, Multihued Immigrant Population Raises Question of What Being 'Canadian' Means Now," *Washington Post*, July 5, 1998.

——, "In Canada, a Tricky Balancing Act; Satisfying Demands of Quebec vs. Other Provinces Requires Solomonic Vision," *Washington Post*, July 16, 1998.

INDEX